RESPECTFUL ATHEISM

A Perspective on Belief in God and Each Other

Thomas B. Sheridan

Prometheus Books

Guilford, Connecticut

 Prometheus Books

An imprint of The Rowman & Littlefield Publishing Group, Inc.
4501 Forbes Boulevard, Suite 200
Lanham, Maryland 20706
www.rowman.com

Distributed by NATIONAL BOOK NETWORK

British Library Cataloguing in Publication Information Available

Library of Congress Cataloging-in-Publication Data

Names: Sheridan, Thomas B., 1929– author.
Title: Respectful atheism : a perspective on belief in God and each other / Thomas B. Sheridan.
Description: Lanham, MD : Prometheus Books, [2021] | Includes bibliographical references and index. | Summary: "This book considers what it means to respect others' beliefs and cultural traditions without abandoning a sincere disbelief in a supernatural being"— Provided by publisher.
Identifiers: LCCN 2020032083 (print) | LCCN 2020032084 (ebook) | ISBN 9781633886605 (cloth) | ISBN 9781633886612 (ebook)
Subjects: LCSH: God. | Religion. | Faith. | Respect for persons. | Atheism.
Classification: LCC BL473 .S43 2021 (print) | LCC BL473 (ebook) | DDC 211/.8—dc23
LC record available at https://lccn.loc.gov/2020032083
LC ebook record available at https://lccn.loc.gov/2020032084

For Nancy and my wonderful family

CONTENTS

PREFACE

This is a book about my faith journey, or—perhaps more accurately—my unfaith journey. The question of God has fascinated me for a long time, and in recent years I have had time to do a lot of reading on all sides of the question.

In 2014, I wrote a book entitled *What Is God? Can Religion Be Modeled?*[1] Its focus is on whether the language of science can be used to represent an abstract concept of God, as contrasted to characterizing the human practice of religion. I used that book for several years to teach a Tufts University adult education course called "Respectful Atheism."[2] The students, an enjoyable spectrum from true believers to nonbelievers, endured my heavy dose of slanted religious history, science, and philosophy. But they repeatedly raised the question that I had mostly ignored: "What about the *respectful* descriptor in the course title?" For them it was a serious question regarding atheism. In other words, does a religious belief that denies the theistic assumptions of various religious traditions have some obligation to respect others' beliefs? Is atheism inherently disrespectful?

This book tackles that question, in addition to laying out a case for not believing in the traditional Western idea of what "God" means. Clearly there are many variants of this belief. To deal adequately with the God question, the book necessarily draws on most of the same history of religion and the same philosophy of knowledge and science as was covered in the earlier book. In the current book, there is much less emphasis on scientific modeling and much new material dealing with the "respectful" question. In that sense, this book is a major revision of the earlier one but with a very different slant.

I have found the concept of God to be questionable, and also troubling, and clearly I am not alone. I am troubled because not only does the traditional idea of God that most people appear to hold seem so incompatible with science, but also throughout history God has been the justification for killing and mayhem on a grand scale, and that same tradition is alive and well today. What has also puzzled me is that many people, including many of those who make a profession of religion, refer to God as though they know what or who God *is* and imply that others know what is meant by the term. Maybe I'm being picky, but I never have been so graced.

In case you wondered, I have not been unchurched. I was raised in a midwestern Presbyterian church and since marriage have been active in a New England Congregational Church. There I was a deacon and served two stints as moderator, the lay leader of the congregation. I have lectured to the World Council of Churches and in retirement convened a monthly discussion group on the subject of God and religious belief. I can still be an atheist, as I argue here. I call myself a "Christian atheist," as so many of the teachings of Jesus and the Abrahamic traditions do speak to me.

ACKNOWLEDGMENTS

I am indebted to the students in my various seminars on this subject for their diverse views and keen observations, which taught me so much. I also want to declare my debt to late professor Neville Moray for numerous e-mail exchanges regarding points of philosophy in which he was so much better versed than myself.

INTRODUCTION

What is meant by *respectful atheism*? Atheism, first, is a belief that what most people call God does not exist. More specifically, atheism usually refers to disbelief in the traditional idea of an all-powerful, all-knowing, loving being who observes and cares for each individual person, and occasionally intercedes in our lives. There are, of course, many variants on that traditional conception. A respectful atheist recognizes and appreciates that different people have different beliefs that they have come to because of family, community, education, contemplation, or other aspects of their experience. A respectful atheist acknowledges everyone's right to their own beliefs, so long as they do not take destructive action against others who believe differently.

A family member once asked whether my chosen book title, *"respectful* atheism," was meant to mean *"respectable* atheism." Good question, since throughout history many folks have regarded atheism as being not socially approved and not morally correct, and therefore disrespectable. Related philosophical arguments made by atheists are seen not to respect the long-standing and deeply ingrained traditions of belief in God. In other words, atheism is seen to be *disrespectable* primarily because it is *disrespectful* of traditional belief. Tit for tat. This is a serious question that is addressed later in this book.

A PREVALENT REACTION TO THE "NEW ATHEISTS"

The term "new atheists" has been used to refer to a group of authors whose recent books have caused quite a stir because of the directness with which they declare their atheism—in contrast to gentler atheism proposals and skepticism made by numerous other authors throughout history dating back to the ancient Greeks.

Prominent among those called the "new atheists" are the following:

Evolutionist Richard Dawkins, author of the books *The God Delusion*, *The Selfish Gene*, and *The Blind Watchmaker* (Dawkins is probably the most famous of the new atheists.)

Neuroscientist Sam Harris, author of *The End of Faith*, *Letter to a Christian Nation*, and *The Moral Landscape*

Philosopher Daniel C. Dennett, author of *Breaking the Spell*

Editor Christopher Hitchens, author of *God Is Not Great* and *The Portable Atheist*

Physicist Victor Stenger, author of *God, the Failed Hypothesis*

I refer to these authors, their books, and their perspectives to address various key questions later in this book.

Some degree of resentment, even hatred, seems to have developed from a cadre of folks who are critical of the so-called new atheists and their message. An example of such a reaction is evident in a new book by Anthony DeStefano, author of *A Traveler's Guide to Heaven*, *Ten Prayers God Always Says Yes To*, and other books on religion, including multiple children's books. His new book, *Inside the Atheist Mind*,[1] is endorsed by Mike Huckabee, Glen Beck, and Rick Santorum. Chapter titles are as follows: "The Arrogance of the Atheists"; "The Ignorance of the Atheists"; "The Ruthlessness of the Atheists"; "The Intolerance of the Atheists"; "The Shallowness of the Atheists"; "The Cowardice of the Atheists'; "The Death-Centeredness of the Atheists"; "The Faithfulness of the Atheists"; "The Malevolence of the Atheists"; and "The End of the Atheists." The chapter headings give a strong hint of the content. Stefano carefully selects figures from history who claimed to be believers. (Of course, almost everyone was. Dissent could result in death—recall Socrates and Galileo.) DeStefano avoids citing the historical skeptics. He points out the many deaths caused by "atheistic rulers such as Hitler and

Stalin" without mentioning the Crusades and other holy wars. (Actually, Hitler, in his *Mein Kampf*, professes love of God many times.)

DiStefano asserts that atheists today are simplistic, militant, intolerant, dogmatic, evangelistic, and irrational.[2] So how does he expect atheists to react to his charges? What about that first principle of Christianity, Judaism, and many other religious traditions about loving one's neighbor? DeStefano's rage against disbelievers seems to belie a deep sense of fear that increasingly more scientists and other thinkers are professing atheism, or at least agnosticism, especially in countries and among peoples that are industrialized and have higher levels of education. In this book we will examine the demographic trends.

Consider a report by Lee Billings in *Scientific American* in March 2019, quoting a Dartmouth physicist named Marcel Gleiser, who just won the Templeton Prize. This prize is an annual award of the John Templeton Foundation, which promotes the idea that religion and science are fully compatible (I will say more on that controversial issue later).

> To me, science is one way of connecting with the mystery of existence. And if you think of it that way, the mystery of existence is something that we have wondered about ever since people began asking questions about who we are and where we come from. So while those questions are now part of scientific research, they are much, much older than science. . . . As a theoretical physicist and also someone who spends time out in the mountains, this sort of questioning offers a deeply spiritual connection with the world, through my mind and through my body. Einstein would have said the same thing, I think, with his cosmic religious feeling. . . . I believe we should take a much humbler approach to knowledge, in the sense that if you look carefully at the way science works, you'll see that yes, it is wonderful—magnificent!—but it has limits. And we have to understand and respect those limits. And by doing that, by understanding how science advances, science really becomes a deeply spiritual conversation with the mysterious, about all the things we don't know. So that's one answer to your question. And that has nothing to do with organized religion, obviously, but it does inform my position against atheism. I consider myself an agnostic. . . .
>
> I honestly think atheism is inconsistent with the scientific method. What I mean by that is, what is atheism? It's a statement, a categorical statement, that expresses belief in nonbelief: Namely, "I don't believe even though I have no evidence for or against, simply I don't believe." Period. It's a declaration. But in science we don't really do declara-

tions. We say, "Okay, you can have a hypothesis, you have to have some evidence against or for that." And so an agnostic would say, "Look, I have no evidence for God or any kind of god. What god, first of all? The Maori gods, or the Jewish or Christian or Muslim God? Which god is that?" But on the other hand, an agnostic would acknowledge no right to make a final statement about something he or she doesn't know about. The absence of evidence is not evidence of absence, and all that. This positions me very much against all of the "new atheist" guys—even though I want my message to be respectful of people's beliefs and reasoning, which might be community-based, or dignity-based, and so on.[3]

ATHEIST VERSUS AGNOSTIC

Gleiser makes a beautiful statement; however, I would take issue with his use of the word "atheist" and whether atheism is inconsistent with the scientific method. He is quite correct that absence of evidence is not evidence of absence. In other words, one cannot logically prove that there is no God, even though no evidence, credible in a scientific sense (more on that later), has ever shown up. And, as Dawkins has maintained, if any such evidence ever were to appear, it would turn all of science upside down. In the same manner, one cannot prove that there is no pink unicorn or tooth fairy somewhere. So if one wants to argue that being an atheist means 100 percent certainty that no evidence could ever possibly exist, then no one could legitimately use the term. In that extremist sense I would have to go along with him and claim to be an agnostic.

But it seems to me that if one is 99.9 percent sure there is no God (of the type cited here, namely, the traditional all-powerful, all-knowing, loving being who observes and cares for each individual person), then use of the term "atheist" seems to be entirely appropriate. After all, that is precisely the way science claims to work: It employs inferential statistics, a null hypothesis. The null hypothesis is a statement or default position that there is no relationship between two measured phenomena or conditions (e.g., Nature exists and God exists), in which lack of relationship is assumed to be true until statistical evidence indicates otherwise. The physicists at the Large Hadron Collider in Geneva examined millions of particle collisions and finally had to reject the null hypothesis to "prove" that the Higgs boson existed. No such data have even been sufficient to reject the null hypothesis that God does not exist; therefore, I regard the term "atheist" to be appropriate for all commonsense uses where one is quite confident in one's disbelief and in keeping with the methods of science.

WHY IS THE CONCEPT OF GOD IMPORTANT?

The concept of God is important because so many people think it is and have done so for so long—since the beginning of recorded history. In Western religions, one day of the week is set aside to worship, and in Islam, prayer is required several times every day. God expressions figure often in our everyday lives:

> God is great (Allah Akbar)
> God almighty
> God the father
> God the son
> God the holy spirit (holy ghost)
> God's will
> God willing
> Creator God
> Loving God
> In God we trust
> So help me God
> One nation under God
> God damn
> God everlasting
> All God's children
> God bless you and God bless America (at the end of every American
>   presidential speech)

The assumed presence of God in our lives arises from deeper wellsprings. God has motivated much our culture—our literature, music, and the arts. God is traditionally viewed as the creator of everything, the basis of morality, the supreme authority. God is the ultimate raison d'être.

And yet, in the name of God, wars have been fought throughout history, often concerning only slightly different interpretations of the concept. In the present day, Christian churches, Jewish synagogues, and Islamic mosques are bombed, and worshipers massacred, by hateful shooters with automatic weapons.

Many people have claimed the right to make pronouncements on behalf of God. They have devoted their working lives to God and/or died as martyrs to their beliefs about God. The concept of God is an engine of human history.

DIFFICULTIES OF DISCOURSE ABOUT GOD

In Western culture today, the subject of God is a conversation-stopper. These days one can talk sex, politics, or just about anything else, but in polite company, and *especially* among educated people, it is frequently uncomfortable, impolite, or even threatening to bring up the subject of God. In some cultures, both in the West and elsewhere, only trained authorities (theologians) are entitled to discuss the nature of God. *Theology* derives from Greek *theos* (God) and *logos* (reasoned discourse, according to the Greek philosophical tradition).[4] It is that *reasoning* aspect of theology that we will examine critically.

To begin with, the topic of God does not easily accommodate rational discourse. "God" has many meanings. In some ancient cultures the gods were thought of as special people and animals. In the mainstream of monotheism, at one extreme we have a theistic God: an omniscient, omnipotent, omnibenevolent personal God who loves and cares about all creatures and hears their prayers. Thus, many believers envision an anthropomorphic God: an old, bearded, robed male figure surrounded by angels bringing humankind into existence by a miraculous touch, as in Michelangelo's famous painting on the ceiling of the Sistine Chapel (see figure 0.1).

At another extreme is a *deistic* God, an entity that created the universe but then retreated to letting the universe run on its own, never intervening in human affairs or altering the laws of nature. Deism, which first appeared in the seventeenth century during the Enlightenment, rejects the supernatural (except for a Designer of the initial creation) and any need for revelation.[5] The Deistic concept of God might be depicted by the Kanisza square illusion, as in figure 0.2, where the square is not physically present but is implied or imagined.

Figure 0.1. **Michelangelo's painting on the ceiling of the Sistine Chapel.** *Wikimedia Commons*

To make matters more complex, God has been defined as "no thing" (but not nothing) and being timeless. For us creatures who live in a world of things and time, thinglessness and timelessness make conceiving the state of God (what God *is*) difficult. That difficulty for understanding will be evident in the discussion to come and is one reason I later bring forward questions about whether God is even representable in science-based rationality; however, most of what has been written about God in more recent times are arguments about the process of coming to belief, coming to faith, and exercising that belief and faith, rather than a discussion about what God is.

As with God, atheism also must have many meanings. Which version of God is not believable? Based on the Greek roots of the term (*a*, meaning without, and *theos*, meaning God), philosopher Michael Martin suggests that the term "negative atheism" be used for having an absence of belief in God. For the more common meaning, a belief that there is no God or gods, he suggests the term "positive atheism." Both terms are to be distinguished from "agnosticism," the position of neither believing nor disbelieving (from the Greek: "without knowledge"). [6]

Figure 0.2. The Kanisza square illusion. Not physically present but implied by sensed reality. *Author's drawing*

"Spirituality" is a term that means something different to just about everyone. It can refer to churchgoing, prayer, or other religious practice. Or it can refer to private meditation or contemplation, quiet reflection on nature, yoga, absorption in music, etc., completely exclusive and apart from worship of God or participation in any organized religion. As the term is normally used there is clear evidence for spirituality in humans, including atheists. In addition, there are reports of out-of-body experiences (associated with illness and near death, as well as ingestion of drugs) that are sometimes called spiritual. That term receives much more attention in this book.

The historical fact is that the existence of God, in whatever form and understanding, is a tacit belief in Western and much of world culture. Right up to the present time discussions of God tend to start with that existence assumption and go on from there. As contrasted to how *people behave* in worship, after God has been assumed, the question, "What exactly *is* God?" whether we can conceive of a model for God, demands to be asked.

WHAT IS IN THE BOOK

This book consists of an introduction plus four major parts and a conclusion. Each of these parts has numbered chapters on related topics. The first part is entitled "History of Belief," certainly not a balanced history of religion, but instead a more focused discussion on the concept of God and the gradual evolution of skepticism in belief—starting with the gods from ancient Egyptian, Greek, and Roman times through the mid-twentieth century, mostly in the Western world. Before moving on to current times I purposely interrupt the flow with a second part titled "Knowledge, Science, and Modeling." The purpose of this part is to remind the reader of the post-Enlightenment notions that now moderate serious thinking about our universe and what we can properly know or believe, and the languages we use to talk about it. I include several sections on "modeling," which normally means the representation of specific things or events in scientific denotative language, as contrasted to the connotative language of myth, metaphor, poetry, and art (which are just as or perhaps more important than what we "know" from science). I show that the abstract concept of God is not amenable to modeling in denotative terms, whereas the human behavior of practicing religion certainly can be modeled that way.

The third part, "Belief Today," includes a variety of topics that describe the current situation as I see it. It includes discussion of demographic trends on belief; the "new atheism"; new physical ideas about the origins of our universe; comments on the importance of metaphor, myth, and religious language in the experience of spirituality; and some questions about the behavior of churchgoers. It also includes a dialog between two famous advocates, one for God and the other for atheism. Finally, it poses a new definition of God, what it should mean to respect that God, to love one's neighbor, and to be in awe of humanity, nature, and the universe.

The fourth and final part is entitled "Respecting Others." In this section I ask what it means to respect others—especially whether and how an atheist can respect other religious perspectives. It includes chapters on compassion, moral virtues, reverence, trust, ignorance, and innovation. It poses the difficult "trade-off" problem of respecting others' beliefs as being sincere conclusions based on their legitimate experiences, while at the same time disagreeing with their particular arguments. In the conclusion, I restate the essential ingredients to calling one's self a "respectful (and hopefully respectable) atheist."

Part I

History of Belief

I

ORIGINS OF BELIEF

There is only one God, knowledge, and one evil, ignorance.—Diogenes Laertius, *Lives of Eminent Philosophers*, 1–5, c. 400 BC

What is it: Is man only a blunder of God, or is God only a blunder of man?—Friedrich Wilhelm Nietzsche, *The Twilight of the Idols*, 1889

History is a description of how as people we came to be what we are, including how we came to believe what we believe; therefore, it seems appropriate to review the history of belief. I do not claim what follows to be an evenhanded rendering of such a history. There are hundreds of works that do that job much better than I can in a very terse treatment. I can only summarize what seem to me to be the highlights of theistic belief, *as well as those of skepticism*. That is meant to provide a precursor to modern thinking about God and support my own comfort with disbelief.

Furthermore, what is reviewed here relates mostly to the development of Abrahamic religions in Western countries. Based on my own ignorance of Indic, East Asian, Middle Eastern, and indigenous traditions of Africa I have omitted those developments.

EARLIEST IDEAS ABOUT GODS

According to mythology and cave drawings, ancient Egypt had 60 to 100 gods and goddesses, who were believed to be present in nature, between

3000 BC and 100 AD.[1] The myths about these gods explained the origins and behavior of various elements in nature. The practices of Egyptian religion were efforts to provide for the gods and gain their favor.

Egyptian religious practice was centered on the pharaoh, the king. Although he was a human, he was believed to be descended from the gods and acted as the intermediary between his people and the gods. There was an obligation to please the gods through rituals and offerings to keep order in the universe. According to one charming myth,

> At first there was only Nun. Nun was the dark waters of chaos. One day a hill rose out of the waters. This hill was called Ben-Ben. On this hill stood Atum, the first god. Atum coughed and spat out Shu, the god of the air, and Tefnut, the goddess of moisture. Shu and Tefnut had two children. First, there was Geb, the god of the earth. Then, there was Nut, the goddess of the sky. Shu lifted Nut up so that she became a canopy over Geb. Nut and Geb had four children named Osiris, Isis, Seth, and Nephthys. Osiris was the king of the earth, and Isis was the queen. Osiris was a good king, and he ruled over the earth for many years; however, everything was not well. Seth was jealous of Osiris because he wanted to be the ruler of the earth. He grew angrier and angrier until one day he killed Osiris. Osiris went down into the underworld, and Seth remained on earth and became king. Osiris and Isis had one son called Horus. Horus battled against Seth and regained the throne. After that, Horus was the king of the earth, and Osiris was the king of the underworld.[2]

With succeeding pharaohs many other gods came into prominence. Ra, the sun god, became the most important. From a purely rational perspective, one might assert that worship of the sun made a lot of sense since the sun provides heat and light, energy to grow crops, etc. The sun is essential to our survival. It was obvious, consistent, and satisfying that the sun god traveled across the sky by day and traversed hades by night, to reappear reliably the next day. Ra is pictured in figure 1.1.

Both the Greek empire (dating from roughly 800 BC) and the Roman empire (dating from the founding of Rome by Romulus in 753 BC) had their panoply of gods. There are many names for what appear to be the same gods. Popular names and corresponding functions for the Greek gods are as follows, with the Roman equivalent in parentheses:

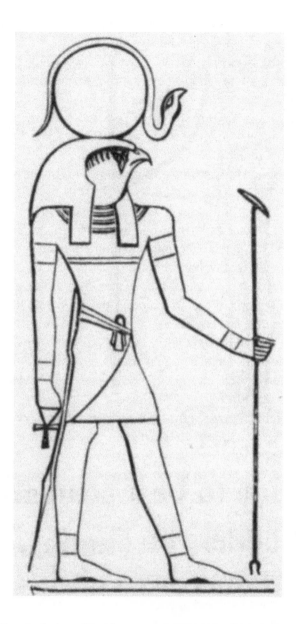

Figure 1.1. One depiction of Ra, the sun god. *Wikimedia Commons*

Zeus (Jupiter): Lord of the sky and supreme ruler of the gods. Known for throwing lightning bolts.

Poseidon (Neptune): Ruler of the sea. Brother of Zeus. Carried a three-pronged spear known as a trident.

Hades (Pluto): Ruler of the underworld and the dead. Brother of Zeus.
Had a helmet that rendered its wearer invisible.

Hestia (Vesta): A virgin goddess. Sister of Zeus. No distinct personality or part in myths. Goddess of the Hearth, the symbol of the home.

Hera (Juno): Zeus's wife and sister. Protector of marriage. Spent most of her time punishing the many women Zeus fell in love with. Liked cows and peacocks.

Ares (Mars): God of war. Son of Zeus and Hera. Liked vultures and dogs.

Athena (Minerva): Daughter of Zeus alone. No mother. She sprang from Zeus's head full-grown and in full armor. The protector of civilized life, handicrafts, and agriculture. She invented the bridle and was the first to tame the horse.

Apollo (Apollo): Son of Zeus. Master musician, archer god, healer, god of light, god of truth, sun god. A busy god who liked the laurel tree, dolphins, and crows.

Aphrodite (Venus): Daughter of Zeus. Goddess of love and beauty. Liked the myrtle tree, doves, sparrows, and swans.

Hermes (Mercury): Son of Zeus. Wore wings on his sandals and hat, and thus was graceful and swift.

Artemis (Diana): Apollo's twin sister and daughter of Zeus. Lady of wild things and huntsman to the gods. As Apollo is the Sun, Artemis is the moon.

Hephaestus (Vulcan): Son of Hera, the god of fire. The only ugly and deformed god. Made armor and weapons forged under volcanoes.

Gaea (Terra): Mother Earth.

Asclepius (Aesculapius): God of medicine.

Cronus (Saturn): God of the sky. Ruler of the Titans. (Roman mythology: God of agriculture.)

Demeter (Ceres): Goddess of grain.

Dionysus (Bacchus): God of wine and vegetation.

Eros (Cupid): God of love.

Hypnos (Somnus): God of sleep.

Rhea (Ops): Wife of Cronus/Saturn. Mother Goddess.

Uranus (Uranus): God of the sky. Father of the Titans.

Nike (Victoria): Goddess of victory.[3]

Starting with the ancient Egyptians through the Greek and Roman gods, all were anthropomorphic (humanlike), although some also had features of animals. That was well ingrained in the notion of what a god was. To be other than creature-like was not imaginable.

The early Persian empire (550–330 BC) also had its large cadre of gods.[4] Every worldly object had a counterpart in the complex sacred world. In Arabic, al-Lah, the supreme being, is masculine. The divine and inscrutable essence of God al-Dhat is feminine. Babylonians and Aryans were aware that their myths were not facts but expressed a mystery. Reason was not denied but was transcended. Ancient Persian philosopher Zoroaster (also known as Zarathustra, approximately 630–650 BC), who helped unite the Persian empire, rejected the old multiplicity of gods. He also promoted the idea of a single wise God, Ahura-Mazda, who ruled the entire world. Zoroaster taught that Ahura-Mazda was constantly fighting Ahriman, the spirit of darkness and evil. If you lived a virtuous life you would go to heaven after death. Otherwise you would be punished in hell. Eventually the world would see eternal goodness and peace. Zoroaster's teaching became the basis of the Persian Bible, the *Avesta*.

In Greece, Pythagoras (570–495 BC), aside from his great mathematical achievements, believed that the soul was a fallen god in a human body and that the body was reincarnated again and again into humans, animals, or vegetables, ultimately to become immortal again.[5] Plato (428–348 BC) and his teacher, Socrates, were both influenced by Pythagoras, and often spoke about the nature of wisdom and beauty (which they called eternal "forms"), attributes that later became close to how God was defined.[6]

According to Aristotle (384–322 BC), the eternal forms had reality insofar as they existed in concrete objects in the world.[7] There was a hierarchy of forms, at the top of which was the unmoved mover God, which consisted of pure thought. This god could have little impact on individual lives.

The Jews had already been uniting around the idea of a single personal God, Yahweh. The Moabite Stone, dating to 840 BC, first mentions Yahweh (abbreviated YHWH). Yahweh was a contrast to the gods of the Greeks, Romans, and Hindus, which had human attributes but were otherwise distant and impersonal.

Jesus (7–2 BC to 30–36 AD) was a Jewish carpenter/teacher in Roman Judea. A number of overlapping attributes were that he was a rabbi, healer, social reformer, rabble-rouser, sage and philosopher, and self-described messiah (a savior/liberator). Because of his political protests and success in generating social unrest, he became a thorn in the side of the local Roman administration and was crucified on orders from the Roman prelate, Pontius Pilate. History supports these statements as fact; however, that he was born of a virgin, was the son of God, rose from the dead, ascended into heaven and will return, and fulfilled the messianic prophecies of the Hebrew Bible are matters of dispute, certainly among Jews and Muslims, but even among modern Christian scholars.

Within the early Christian community there was controversy concerning whether Jesus was divine. Since Jesus was an obedient human, it was said he could not be God. Emperor Constantine called the synod of bishops to Nicaea on May 20, 325, to settle the disagreement. Although the decision was not unanimous, the resulting Nicene creed made Jesus one in substance with God (as part of the Trinity).[8]

The Hindus already had a kind of trinity in the form of Brahman, Shiva, and Vishnu, who were three aspects of a single God. Today, of course, Muslims take Christians to task for having three gods and assert, "There is no god but God."

JAYNES'S BICAMERAL THEORY ABOUT HEARING GODS

Now we turn to a fascinating but controversial theory about how the voice of God (or gods) impacted ancient man. In 1976, psychologist Julian Jaynes authored a book that posited a theory about how mankind came to be religious. The book is titled *The Origin of Consciousness in the Breakdown of the Bicameral Mind*.[9] The term "bicameral" (literally, two chambers) refers to the two distinct hemispheres of the cerebrum connected through the corpus callosum. In addition to the left hemisphere receiving neural signals from the right side of the body, as well as sending neural signals to the right side of the body, and the right hemisphere receiving neural signals from the left side of the body, as well as sending neural signals to the left side of the body, there is also further specialization. The left hemisphere is thought to control audible speech and writing, whereas the right hemisphere excels at spatial and nonverbal tasks. It is said that the left side is "analytic" and "logical," whereas the right side is "holistic" and "intuitive." Obviously, many, if not most, functions involve both sides.

The gist of Jaynes's radical idea is that consciousness, subjectivity, awareness of self, the ego, the ability to introspect, and autobiographical memory originated in mankind only 3,000 years ago. Prior to that people were driven by auditory hallucinations, what they considered to be the gods talking to them and telling them what to do, particularly in situations of stress. The voices of kings (they were gods, too) were also heard, even after their deaths. The voice hallucinations were not imagination, but the manifestation of man's volitions. Experiences originating in the right hemisphere were transmitted to the language centers in the left hemisphere, namely, Wernicke's area and Broca's area.

Jaynes is no slouch when it comes to ancient history. He reviews in great detail what we know about these hallucinations from such ancient writings as the *Iliad* and the Hebrew Bible, and other relics from Mesopotamia, ancient Greece, Peru, etc. So, Jaynes's theory is that early man believed that the second voice that he was hearing, which directed him in times of stress, was the voice of a god. But in about 1000 BC, man became aware that the voice was his own: He became self-conscious. Consciousness is not an easy topic. Philosophers have pondered the subject for a long time and have as yet no simple answers. One can say consciousness is a process rather than a thing, but that seems not to help much. We do observe that much of our behavior is automatic, not driven by conscious will. When we do think consciously, we tend to think and understand in metaphors. An example is time. The particular metaphor we use is space. Time goes from left to right. We also tend to use narrative, a mental description of a sequence of events to make sense to ourselves. Jaynes's claim is that prior to 1000 BC, this kind of processing either did not exist or existed in a form much more primitive than what we experience today by introspection.

Primitive peoples had speech, but writing came later. Speech was converted to writing only 3,000 years ago. The earliest writing was done to keep inventory of food, arms, etc. But, Jaynes asserts, certain ideas we now take for granted were originally missing. For example, a word for "mental will" is absent in Homer's *Iliad* (eighth century BC). But they surely had words for gods. Gradually, writing included narratives of god-related events, descriptions of when and where voices of gods were heard. Then, along with writing and storytelling, there came a weakening of the importance of the gods appearing in auditory form. And there was recognition of the chaos and suffering of the period (Trojan wars and earthquakes throughout the Mediterranean area in about 1200 BC). Earlier there had been no need for prayer and supplication to the gods since the gods were obviously in control, but now all the chaos made the gods seem to be missing. Various rituals and intermediaries (angels and demons) were invented to help counteract the confusing violence and apparent malevolence of the gods and gain access to them. Human prophets were recognized. There were new efforts to divine the speech of the now-silent gods. Words for spirit, soul, and mind appeared (e.g., "psyche" from the Greek).

While originally there were only words relating to external events, new words relating to internal sensations appeared, then mental processes, then introspection. For example, in Amos, which some scholars claim is the oldest chapter of the Hebrew Bible, originally written in approximately 800 BC, there are no such words, and similarly for Jeremiah and Ezekiel. Ecclesiastes, the newest chapter (200 BC), does have words for pondering and spatialization of time, and for seeking wisdom, not just from the authoritarian Yahweh. Sacred texts in India changed during a similar period, from the *Vedas* (*sruti*, or directly revealed, "what is heard") to the much more subjective *Upanishads* (consisting of human commentary). Jaynes refers often to the rise, at the time of the bicameral shift, of what he calls the "analog I." By this he distinguishes the linguistic term of self-reference from the actual person and claims that prior to the bicameral shift no such terminology was in use, i.e., the concept of "I" was not available.

Jaynes recounts numerous connections of modern religions to the ancient bicameral absolutes (and away from the somewhat more difficult agape). There is a seeming desire to make contact with the lost authority in the unsubjective bicameral past. For example, the ancient oracle priestesses (sibyls) who operated under influence of the gods are found on the ceiling of Michelangelo's Sistine Chapel. Even today statues and paintings of the Virgin Mary are claimed to shed tears. There are cults that speak in tongues and hold training sessions to bring on trances so as to become possessed, all in submission to an authoritarian God that can talk through them. Modern religious rituals invoke procedures that incorporate other compelling attributes of expectancy and authority.

Jaynes devotes considerable discussion to poetry. It is interesting that in bicameral times the gods supposedly spoke in poetry rather than prose: the Oracle of Delphi, the Indian *Vedas*, the prophets of Yahweh. The *Iliad* is written in poetry, and the trend simply continued as the bicameral mind broke down. The *Bhagavad Gita* and other writings of the later period are in poetry.[10] Speech is primarily in the left hemisphere, but poetry, which is much closer to song (music), is in the right. Jaynes suggests that music may have been invented as a "neural expectant to the hallucination of the gods" in the absence of self-consciousness. His idea is that the continuance of poetry and music resulted from the "change from a divine given" to a human activity based on nostalgia for the absolute. There is no question that sacred music still inspires and conjures feelings of awe.

Because of the obvious connections to his notions of the bicameral mind, Jaynes cannot avoid the topics of hypnosis and schizophrenia. The history of hypnosis is littered with bizarre accounts, including Anton Messner's claim that hypnosis is a human-to-human gravitational attraction that accords with Newton's gravity. Accordingly, he fed subjects iron to see if they became attracted to one another, but mostly got convulsive behavior. But we know that teaching of expectations (prior statements of how subjects would behave) and focusing of attention (by having subjects stare at a light or voluntarily attend to only the voice of the authority figure) can bring on a hypnotic state. Jaynes suggests that this activates right brain domination over left brain ego control.

Schizophrenia is claimed to be uniquely consistent with the bicameral mind—a partial relapse to that primitive state. It is said to be accompanied by a failure of coherent narrative ability, hallucination, erosion of the ego, and, in certain cases, breakdown of a body image (or connection between self and environment).

Jaynes concludes his treatise by asserting that science itself can be read as a breakdown of the bicameral mind in a search for a hidden divinity: "God is right out here under the stars to be talked about and heard brilliantly in all the grandeur of reason, rather than behind the rood screen of ignorance in the murky mutterings of costumed priests."[11] Poetically put.

Jaynes's book provoked much controversy when it was first published and remains a theory for psychologists, psychiatrists, and neuroscientists to contend with. One picking point is that a story called *The Epic of Gilgamesh*, reported to predate the Hebrew Bible, does exhibit features of introspection. But Jaynes has countered that a more complete version of the story that was discovered in post bicameral times does not really contain significant introspection.

Recent neuroimaging studies tend to support Jaynes by providing new evidence of hallucinations that arise in the right temporal-parietal lobe and are transmitted through the corpus callosum to the left temporal lobe. Modern brain imaging techniques, particularly PET (positron emission tomography) and functional MRI (magnetic resonance imaging), which reveal local brain activity, will no doubt have much more to say about bicameralism in the future.[12] Philosopher Daniel Dennett comments that this *divination* was primitive man's way to avoid self-control and pass the buck to something that can be held responsible if things don't go well.

We have seen that, assuming the Jaynes theory has credibility, primitive peoples experienced a kind of virtual reality, a virtual authoritarian presence that was ascribed to divinity (there being no other evident reason for the inner voices). Furthermore, according to Jaynes, mankind has retained vestiges of that virtual reality right up to modern times. We will come back to virtual reality in a later chapter.

THE FIRST SKEPTICS

Protagoras (ca. 490–420 BC) was the first Greek philosopher known to have explicitly implied agnosticism. In his work *Concerning the Gods*, he asserts, "I am unable to discover whether they exist or not, or what they are like in form." In the tragic play *Bellerophon*, possibly performed in the fifth century BC, there are the words, "Does someone say there are indeed gods in heaven? There are not, there are not, if a man is willing not to rely foolishly on the antiquated reasoning." In the play *On Piety* by playwright Cretius, the principal actor tells how "someone first persuaded mortals to believe that there exists a race of gods."[13]

We know that Socrates (469–399 BC) left no written works; however, his questioning about the gods is known through his students. For example, Plato (428–347 BC), in his *Apology*, says of Socrates' accusers, "Those who hear them suppose that anyone who inquires into such matters must be an atheist." In 399 BC, the Athenians formally charged Socrates: "Socrates does wrong by not acknowledging the gods the city acknowledges and introducing other, new powers. He also does wrong by corrupting the young." Socrates was eventually sentenced to death by drinking the hemlock, and there followed a period when not only the Greek philosophers, but also the Romans, Jews, and Christians avoided openly doubting that the gods existed and referred to any doubters as atheists.

Siddhartha Gautama, the Buddha, (in about 450 BC) taught that one's sense of transcendence in meditation is not contact with a god but with oneself. It was agreed that asking a Buddhist about life after death is simply improper, since the answer was beyond any human understanding.

In early Christianity, Mark's gospel was the earliest and therefore probably the most reliable.[14] He implied that Jesus was a normal person growing up. Jesus never claimed to be God, but he spoke of God in seemingly personal terms as a loving father. Plotinus (205–270), in contrast, described God as everything and nothing, beyond all human categories. Already there were very opposite descriptions of what/who God was.

DEVELOPMENT OF DIFFERENT RELIGIOUS TRADITIONS

Augustine of Hippo (354–430) is one of the greatest Christian thinkers. He profoundly influenced the medieval worldview, particularly within the Catholic Church. He defined Trinity for the Latin church and is also considered to be a father of the reformation due to his teachings on salvation and divine grace. Augustine believed that humanity was damned because of Adam and Eve's sin (guilt passed on through their sexual encounter) but has been redeemed by the death and resurrection of Jesus. Where Christianity originally regarded women positively, Augustine believed their only function was childbearing. It is recorded that he prayed, "Lord, give me chastity, but not yet."[15]

In about 610, an Arab merchant named Muhammad is said to have had a vision of the angel Gabriel on a mountain, receiving throughout time all the words in what we now know to be the Quran.[16] Allegedly, he remembered it perfectly and later recited it so that scribes could record it. By the time of his death in 632, he had united almost every tribe in Arabia into a united community (an *ummah*). The first official compilation of the Quran was 20 years after Muhammad died. The Quran emphasizes surrender (Islam) to al-Lah, a moral imperative. It dismisses theological speculation about ideas of Trinity and incarnation as self-indulgence and guesswork.

Most of the Prophet Muhammad's followers wanted the community of Muslims to determine who would succeed him. A group called the Shia thought that someone from his family should take up his mantle. They favored Ali, who was married to Muhammad's daughter, Fatimah. Sunnis believed that leadership should fall to the person who was deemed by the elite of the community to be best able to lead the community. And it was fundamentally that political division that began the Sunni–Shia split. The Sunnis prevailed and chose a successor to be the first caliph. Eventually, Ali was chosen as the fourth caliph, but not before violent conflict broke out. Two of the earliest caliphs were murdered. War erupted when Ali became caliph, and he too was killed in fighting in 661.[17]

Later, in the ninth century, a new type of Islam emerged (falsafah), agreeing with the Greeks in emphasizing a continuous search for wisdom through reason, since God was said to be the same as reason. The Muslims began to accept the monotheistic God of the ancients as the same God as al-Lah. But the Muslim sects continue to disagree with one another. The Shia caliphate in Tunis (later Cairo) was opposed to the Sunni caliphate in Baghdad. Shii believed imams were special in their perfect surrender to God, much as were Jesus and Moses.

The period from 1096–1099 saw the first Christian crusade against the infidel Jews and Muslims.[18] Soldiers fought under the banner of St. George, seeing Jesus as a feudal lord. They sought to recover Jesus' patrimony and honor.

The Greeks had always distrusted Augustine's Trinity. Greek theology was contemplation of the mystery of Trinity and incarnation. The Latins made it too comprehensible and rational. Christians started adopting falsafah just when Greeks were losing faith in it. Rabbi Moses ibn Maimon (Maimonides, 1135–1204) believed that the highest knowledge of God derived more from imagination than intellect.

Thomas Aquinas (1225–1274), in his *Summa Theologica*, tried to combine the ideas of Augustine and Greek philosophy—namely, the exact nature of God is inaccessible, but certain premises must hold, including that God is a superior and perfect being whose existence is necessary, and who was creator of the cosmos at the beginning of time. He argued five ways to "prove" the existence of God. They boil down to God being (1) the essential first mover that (2) cannot have a prior mover and (3) that is not contingent on another being and (4) is maximally causative and (5) is maximally knowledgeable. He articulated what is now the common description of God as omniscient, omnipotent, and omnibenevolent.

Isaac Luria Ashkenazi (1534–1572) was a foremost rabbi and Jewish mystic in the community of Safed in the Galilee region of Ottoman Palestine, and a hero and saint of Kabbalism.[19] He dwelt on the old question of how a perfect God could create an imperfect world. His answer was that God abandoned part of himself. Luria preached a doctrine of good works and so helped European Jews be positive in their hard times. This was in contrast to Luther and Calvin, who in the same period said salvation was only by grace.

Martin Luther (1483–1546) believed that life was a battle against Satan. God can only be found in suffering, as symbolized by the cross. Faith was a trusting leap in the dark, not any human assent to certain propositions. Luther was a strong anti-Semite and misogynist who had a loathing and horror of sexuality.[20]

John Calvin (1509–1564) inspired the puritan revolutions in England under Cromwell and the colonization of New England. God was believed to be the absolute ruler. But Calvin also believed in predestination, which limited the interactions of a personal God with the people.[21]

René Descartes (1596–1650) reworked Anselm's ontological proof (that God exists because one can think no greater thought). He most famously asserted that the very experience of doubt tells us that the doubter must exist. "I think, therefore I am" was his way of putting it. His proof of God involved a number of premises that will not be reviewed in detail here. But key among these was that one's grasp of the infinite must be prior to one's grasp of the finite and that the idea of God is completely clear and distinct, and contains more objective reality than any other idea.[22]

Blaise Pascal (1623–1662) thought belief in God had to be a matter of subjective choice among alternatives rather than a conclusion from rational deduction. He also went along with Luther and was later supported by Søren Kierkegaard, that belief in God requires a leap of faith.[23]

Isaac Newton (1642–1727) was anxious to rid Christianity of mystery. During the seventeenth century, as the ideas of the Enlightenment became popular, defining God in terms of mystery, myth, and mysticism was seen as a problem that had to be cleared up.[24] At the same time people started calling out those who acted as though God did not exist as "atheists." But literal atheism (disbelief) was unimaginable for most people since religion dominated everyday life.

PANTHEISM: BARUCH SPINOZA

Since it has a special place in forming my own philosophy, I provide special mention of Spinoza. Baruch Spinoza was a Dutch Jew (1632–1677) who was excommunicated from his synagogue at Amsterdam.[25] He has been regarded as a classical pantheist, believing that God and nature are one and the same. His 1670 *Theologico-Political Treatise*, which he published anonymously, was received unfavorably by the philosophers of the day, for example, Leibniz. After Spinoza's death, his works had to be published in secret to avoid confiscation. He was critical of both Catholicism and Islam, claiming that both religions are made "to deceive the people and to constrain the minds of men."

Spinoza argued that God exists and is abstract and impersonal. He believed that God amounted to the sum of all the physical laws; therefore, to say that God must be separated from everything makes no sense, for in that case it would be impossible to say that he exists. Spinoza has been called an epicurean materialist, given that Epicureans believed that atoms and their probabilistic paths were all that existed (in seeming anticipation of modern quantum theory). But Spinoza adhered to strict determinism, in contrast to randomness or "received authority." He contended that "Deus sive Natura" is a being of infinitely many attributes and that there is no separation of mind and body. He rejected mind–body dualism, popular at the time, believing that mind and body are intimately coordinated and part of the same entity (which is essentially the position of modern neuroscience).

Spinoza believed that God does not rule over the universe in the sense that He can and does make changes, and he challenged the idea of a transcendental God that actively responds to events in the universe. Everything that has and will happen is part of a long chain of cause and effect, which humans are unable to change. Thus, no amount of prayer or ritual will sway God. Nevertheless, the highest virtue is the intellectual love or longing for knowledge of God/nature/universe.

Being a strict determinist, Spinoza believed that everything that happens occurs because it must. Nothing happens by chance. Humans have no free will, despite thinking that they do. The perception of freedom is illusory and results from human consciousness, experience, and indifference to prior natural causes. "All believe that they speak by a free command of the mind, whilst in truth they have no power to restrain the impulse which they have to speak." Blame and praise are nonexistent human ideals, only experienced because we are so acclimatized to human consciousness interlinking with our experience that we have a false idea of free choice. If circumstances are seen as unfortunate it is only because of our inadequate conception of reality. Small components in the chain of cause and effect may be understood by human reason, but grasp of the infinite complexity of the whole is fully beyond the capability of empirical science to comprehend.

Later philosophers like Karl Jaspers (1883–1969) have implied that Spinoza did not mean to assert that God and nature are interchangeable ideas, but rather that the finite physical world is subservient to God's infinity of attributes.[26] Martial Gueroult put it that the world is not God, but in a strong sense it is "in" God.

Spinoza was considered an atheist because his concept of God was so different from that of traditional Judeo-Christian theism. Spinoza specifically denied God having personality, intelligence, feeling, or will: He does not act according to purpose, but everything follows necessarily from His nature. This makes God the antithesis of an anthropomorphic fatherly God who cares about humanity. Karl Marx allegedly liked Spinoza's ideas about the universe, interpreting it as materialistic. Nietzsche also esteemed Spinoza. George Santayana regarded Spinoza as a model for understanding the naturalistic basis of morality.

FURTHER DEVELOPMENT OF SKEPTICISM

Aquinas and the Roman church had encouraged the idea that human reason was limited and therefore must be subjected to divine revelation. In contrast, Descartes believed that theological knowledge is not special but must pass the same empirical rationality criteria as used in worldly matters. But as noted earlier, he tried to prove the existence of God by using the traditional argument of St. Anselm of Canterbury (1033–1109) that God must exist because by definition, "No greater being can be conceived"—a position that left him open to criticism on rational grounds.[27]

The arguments of rational empiricism versus mystical reflection went back and forth. John Locke (1632–1704) criticized Descartes's efforts at theological rationality, asserting that the concept of God can only be

derived from "ideas received from sensation and reflection."[28] Henry
More (1614–1687) defined God not as a transcendent mystery, but rather
an infinitely extensible spiritual body, to be distinguished from a solid
body. He saw God as the harmonious sum of everything.[29] David Hume
(1711–1776) confronted the question of God head-on. He made plain that
theism is incompatible with empiricism and that if one reasoned from
known phenomena one would have to drop supposition and conjecture
about God.[30]

Immanuel Kant (1724–1804), in *Critique of Pure Reason*, provides an
erudite and detailed discussion of causality and time precedence.[31] Those
issues were not novel, for Aquinas and others earlier had discussed causality. In fact, the awareness of causality seems to date to pre-Socratic
times when people realized that they themselves were the immediate
causes of events and not the gods. Today we appreciate that temporal
precedence is more complex than what Kant understood, time precedence
depending on arbitrary assignment of what is the cause (e.g., when you
push on a spring does the motion cause the force or does the force cause
the motion?). Today we also appreciate the distinction between *necessity*
(i.e., B occurs *only* if A occurs first or if both A1 and A2 occur) and
sufficiency (B *can* occur if *either* A1 *or* A2 occurs first). With respect to
God, Kant asserted that God would have to be regarded as beyond the
limits of human knowledge. That meant that one would either have to
dispense with God altogether or alternatively believe in a transcendental
God. Kant chose the latter. He was getting closer to a theme of this book,
although in a later section I criticize the notion of a transcendental God.

Denis Diderot (1713–1784) was an openly self-professed and explicit
atheist.[32] He rejected theism in favor of a completely materialistic view of
the universe. He had intellectual stature and so could not be dismissed out
of hand as a fool or a malcontent.

Ludwig Feuerbach (1804–1872) claimed that the prevailing notion of
God was an "incoherent amalgam of personal, quasi-anthropological at-
tributes and impersonal attributes of perfection."[33] He had no use for
Christianity.

It is to Friedrich Nietzsche (1844–1900) that we owe the phrase "God
is Dead" (first used in his book *The Gay Science*).[34] Nietzsche claims that
eliminating God will lead to the rejection of a belief of cosmic or physical
order, and also a rejection of absolute values. This would also be a rejection of belief in an objective and universal moral law binding upon all

individuals. This rejection is called *nihilism*. Nietzsche worked to find a solution for nihilism by rethinking the foundations of human values, foundations that went deeper than Christian values.

The aforementioned very abbreviated recitation of names and beliefs provides a thumbnail historical picture of the struggle of prominent thinkers to resist convention in coping with the question of God's existence.

2

TRADITIONAL "PROOFS" OF GOD

Many of the arguments for the existence of God can be categorized under the philosophical term "ontology," which, as was said earlier, deals with questions concerning what entities exist or can be said to exist. It is closely related to epistemology, which deals with knowing and the methods of obtaining knowledge (like the scientific method).

There is a rich and growing literature on arguments about the existence of God, pros and cons. This brief summary is not meant to be comprehensive, but to provide the gist, in layman's terms, of the main arguments. Each argument for existence is stated succinctly, followed by the popular rebuttal. Some of these arguments are referred to in later discussions about belief.

ANSELM'S THESIS

Probably the earliest argument explicitly offered as "proof" of God's existence was that, as mentioned earlier, offered by Saint Anselm of Canterbury, a Benedictine monk, philosopher, and theologian.[1] His argument was accepted for hundreds of years by the Roman church. In his *Proslogion*, Anselm defines God as "that than which nothing greater can be conceived." In other words, and as stated by Anselm's defenders, if something is so great that it is at the limit of what can be "conceived" (imagined, I assume), then it cannot exist only in thought but must exist in reality because *existence in reality is greater than existence in thought.* Anselm claimed that "only a fool would think otherwise."

Anselm's argument continues to garner attention and be discussed to this day, even though Kant and other philosophers refuted his thesis. I find the Anselm thesis to be contorted logic. Comparing what exists in reality and what exists in thought as to "greatness" seems a strange exercise with no means to validate a judgment. "Greatest" could mean all-inclusive, but that would have to include all that is bad, as well as all that is good. If Anselm meant only all that is good, one would have to ask by whose criteria. God's criteria? But many theologians have implied that we are not party to an understanding of God's criteria. Furthermore, there are lots of things that we readily admit are beyond human understanding (perhaps most things). Anyway, how does that prove the existence of an omnipotent, omniscient, loving God?

On the other hand, I believe Anselm suggests a way to *redefine* God—simply as a way to express what is beyond human understanding—with no need for anything supernatural. This is a very different meaning for God than what is normally assumed. In fact, later I suggest that the term "God" be used in exactly that way. But to define God as the sum of *all* that is beyond human understanding and *nothing more* seems a far cry from the way the term "God" has been used throughout history.

THE COSMOLOGICAL ARGUMENT (FIRST CAUSE)

The cosmological argument is also known as the argument from universal causation or the argument from first cause. It was used by Aristotle in ancient Greece, more with a slant toward physics than theology. In his *Metaphysics*, Aristotle claimed that there must be something to explain why the Universe exists: Causality is linear, so something had to exist first before anything else could exist.[2] He called this an unmoved mover, an uncaused cause. Aquinas took up the Aristotle argument, denying that there can be an infinite causal chain; there must be a stopping point. He stated that even if the universe has always existed, it still owes its existence to an uncaused cause, "and this we understand to be God."

The usual retort to the first cause argument for God is to ask, "What caused God?" British philosopher Samuel Clarke (1675–1729) argued that even if an infinite regressive chain existed, there would have to be a transcendental cause for the entire succession. Hume declared that each step in a causal chain would need a cause, and there is no need to go outside the chain.[3]

ARGUMENT FROM DESIGN (TELEOLOGY)

Teleology means having a purpose. The idea of this argument is that the universe was created for a purpose. The analogy is made to the organs of the human body, each of which has an apparent purpose. So too all the parts of the universe must have a purpose as part of a grand design by God. This argument was put forth by William Paley (1743–1805).[4] Paley pointed out by analogy that a wristwatch has to be designed by a human designer who understands its purpose. The wristwatch design argument for God has been a favorite to rebut by modern Darwinians (cited later).

Critics of this argument raise the question of the gratuitous evil and suffering in the world, which is incompatible with what might be assumed to be actions of a loving God. The counterargument regarding evil in the world devolves with the theist claiming that (1) we are not privy to God's purpose, (2) that God must have His reasons, and that the purpose of life is not necessarily universal happiness, (3) that evil in the world is because mankind has misused the moral freedom God has provided, and (4) that God's purpose carries into eternity and does not end with this transient life.

ARGUMENT FROM MORALITY

The argument here is that God's revealed laws for living set the basis for morality, and without the revelations and worship of God we would have no basis for morality. But then one must ask about so much of what appears immoral in sacred texts, especially the Hebrew Bible. We do not accept worship practices such as sacrifices of children and punishment by death for what today we would regard as minor infractions (examples of this are offered later). Contemporary writer Sam Harris argues that religion is a questionable basis for morality, and suggests that morality has actually evolved over time from what works for the betterment of society.[5]

ARGUMENT FROM MYSTICAL EXPERIENCE

It is common for people to report mystical experiences that seem to have no explanation, and these are attributed to God. The counterargument is that there are many reasons for such experiences, for instance, hallucinations (e.g., the bicameral mind hypothesis of Julian Jaynes cited earlier, as well as dreams, disease, drugs, etc.). Proof of attribution to God would be difficult in any case.

PASCAL'S WAGER

French philosopher-mathematician Blaise Pascal made fundamental contributions to probability theory, as well as physics. In his "wager" (also known as Pascal's gambit) he asserted that everyone, like it or not, is subject to a wager about belief in God's existence: If you believe in God, and God actually exists, Pascal writes in his *Pensees*, you radically improve your chance of going to heaven, and that is for an infinite time (therefore infinite gain). If God exists but you are an atheist, your chances (gain) will be much less, maybe go negative. If God does not exist, whether you believe would make no difference (zero gain); therefore, a rational person will believe in God.[6]

The counter to this argument is that "belief" based on such a wager with one's self would be dishonest for many people who saw no other basis for believing and that a loving God would always wish for one to be intellectually honest. There are also issues with the existence of heaven, who gets to go, and on what terms.

SO MANY PEOPLE BELIEVE

It has been argued that because so many people during a long span of time have believed that God exists, there must be something to it. It's as though history has taken a poll and God wins hands down. A rebuttal is that there are many things that most people believed for a long period of time that turned out not to be true, for example, that the earth is flat.

IT IS NOT POSSIBLE TO DISPROVE THE EXISTENCE OF GOD

It is common for believers to assert that one cannot disprove the existence of God. That is correct; however, such an argument means nothing, since the obligation on anyone asserting God's existence is to prove or otherwise demonstrate the existence. One cannot disprove the existence of anything at some point in space and time; the possibilities for existence are infinite. Bertrand Russell has an interesting commentary on this argument.

> If I were to suggest that between the Earth and Mars there is a china teapot revolving about the sun in an elliptical orbit, nobody would be able to disprove my assertion provided I were careful to add that the teapot is too small to be revealed even by our most powerful telescopes. But if I were to go on to say that, since my assertion cannot be disproved, it is an intolerable assumption on the part of human reason to doubt it, I should rightly be thought to be talking nonsense. If, however, the existence of such a teapot were affirmed in ancient books, taught as the sacred truth every Sunday, and instilled in the minds of children at school, hesitation to believe in its existence would become a mark of eccentricity and entitle the doubter to the attentions of a psychiatrist in an enlightened age or of the inquisitor at an earlier time.[7]

Ludwig Wittgenstein and others have argued for what has been called *epistemic responsibility*, that people have a responsibility to seek evidence for what they believe and that what we cannot speak about (rationally) "we must pass over in silence."[8]

3

MORE RECENT THEISTIC ARGUMENTS

THE MIND–BODY DILEMMA

This argument by the theists is close to (maybe the reverse of) the Anselm argument that inability to imagine the "greatest" something makes it exist. Surely one can say that any imagined thing does exist—in the "mind." Translated into neuroscience that would have to mean that God surely does exist—in the form of nerve impulses and subtle chemical changes in the brain. But then so does any imagined thing exist, a pink unicorn, for example.

The philosophical claim that minds are not distinct from matter (that mental events are experienced counterparts of physical events) is called *physicalism*. Some theists counterargue that God has mental properties but no material properties, and so His existence is incompatible with physicalism. But insofar as mental activity is physical, that argument cannot stand. So most cognitive scientists and neuroscientists subscribe to physicalism to the extent that so-called mind is just a way of talking (loosely) about what we experience with our brains. Surely a person may imagine or hallucinate an object that does not exist outside the brain.

Scientists shy away from scientific investigations that do not have attributes of space and time. Some scientists declare that supernatural phenomena, if they were to exist, necessarily lie beyond the scope of what is knowable to science. So again, science cannot disprove such phenomena, but neither can the theist offer any proof.

Some theists, however, will continue to maintain that physicalism is inherently accepted by the atheist on faith, and so this puts it on an equal footing with accepting God on faith (and maybe also accepting miracles and paranormal phenomena on faith?). And so the mind–body arguments go back and forth, with scientists and theists talking past one another.

ANOTHER EMBELLISHMENT OF THE ANSELM ARGUMENT

Both theist and atheist philosophers like to make erudite verbal statements that at first blush seem to be compelling. For example, theologian William Lane Craig, in reference to God, states,

> A person S is omnipotent at a time t if and only if S can at t actualize any state of affairs that is not described by counterfactuals about the free acts of others and that is broadly logically possible for someone to actualize given the same hard past at t and the same true counterfactuals about free acts of others. [1]

That is philosopher talk that seems to say that if a being can do anything possible that someone else cannot demonstrate, then that person is omnipotent. The rub, of course, comes in showing that those remarkable feats (e.g., creating life) were, in fact, done by that supposed being rather than by some other means.

THERE IS SOMETHING RATHER THAN NOTHING

A question often posed in discussing the origin of the cosmos is why is there something rather than nothing? This apparent fact suggests to some people that only an omnipotent God could create something from nothing. Theist philosopher Richard Swinburne (1934–) asserts that, while science will never be able to solve some problems of science, for instance, why the universe exists, by aggregating many such probabilistic contingencies the existence of God becomes more and more probable; however, in discussing the origin of the universe, physicist Victor Stenger (1935–) notes that in this age of quantum theory, no laws of physics are violated in going from nothing to something.[2] (The proof of that statement is not attempted here.)

NO EVIDENCE IS NECESSARY

Theologist Alvin Plantinga (1932–) argues that no evidence for God is necessary beyond what is self-evident and calls this *foundationalism*.[3] Plantinga claims that the demand for evidential proof is an idea peculiar to Western culture. He believes that some beliefs are primary and self-evident, and need not be derived from prior beliefs. As self-evidence he cites the tendency of believers to feel guilty about being skeptical and then feel forgiven when they repent. Inspiration through reading scripture and the support of a community of religious people also provides self-evidence of God, he claims.

The atheistic response is that accepting these conditions for such basic belief is a bit too easy and that the argument is circular: "I believe in God, therefore it is self-evident that God exists."

BELIEF IN GOD IS SIMPLER THAN WHAT IS REQUIRED FOR DISBELIEF

A slightly different argument by Swinburne is that the hypothesis of theism is much simpler than the hypothesis that a complex physical universe exists as an "uncaused brute fact."[4] He justifies the latter based on the Ockham's razor principle (after 14th-century Franciscan monk William of Ockham).[5] The principle states that when competing hypotheses are equal in other respects, the hypothesis that introduces the fewest assumptions and postulates the fewest entities while still sufficiently answering the question is recommended; however, the claim that the explanation is God, and that this is much simpler than alternative explanations, necessarily involves very complex contingencies.

The sentence "God did it" may be simple, but that's the only thing that is simple. The creationists' assertion that God is the simplest alternative explanation is not simple, but it is simplistic, as "God" is totally undefined—merely a substitute term for what is unknown. In science, Ockham's razor is a *heuristic* (a rule of thumb) to guide scientists in the development of theoretical models, rather than as an arbiter between published models. Ockham's razor is not an irrefutable principle. Nor is it a scientific result. Furthermore, one may question whether Swinburne's assertions meet the criteria of competing hypotheses equal in other respects.

EVOLUTION IS NO SUBSTITUTE FOR GOD'S CREATION

Robert Mackenzie Beverley (1798–1868) accused Darwin of believing that

> absolute ignorance is the artificer, so that we may enunciate as the fundamental principle of the whole system, that, in order to make a perfect and beautiful machine, it is not requisite to know how to make it. By strange inversion of meaning (Darwin) seems to think absolute ignorance is fully qualified to take the place of absolute wisdom in all the creative achievements of creative skill.[6]

The implication is that Darwin's theory cannot possibly substitute for God's creations. This completely misses the essence of Darwin's great idea, where "beautiful machines" emerge from a lengthy evolutionary process in which reproductive capability plus natural environmental forces combine to substitute for the mind of an immediate divine inventor.

PERFECTION ARGUMENT (SECOND LAW OF THERMODYNAMICS)

French biophysicist Pierre Lecomte du Noüy (1883–1947) argued that life, especially the ability to create new life, to continually improve health and age span, etc., defies the second law of thermodynamics. That law of physics says that everything, if left to its own devices, tends toward chaos and degeneration.[7] In other words, life itself defies the second law. So God must be behind life.

Indeed, from a closed system (in space and time) perspective, that might appear to be true. But the counter is that when the totality of the universe and time are considered, the slow succession of stages of evolutionary development, combined with the energy put into the earthly process by the sun, makes life consistent with the second law. One cannot isolate the Earth from the sun in terms of physical interactions.

NO CAUSE IS NECESSARY; GOD EXISTS IN TIMELESS ETERNITY

A theist answer to the challenge of what caused God is simply that God was always there and that the very idea of causality in time is a man-made idea. God is timeless and not subject to having been caused. A counterargument is that man is incapable of rational thought about natural phenomena that do not include time and causality. I say "include" because some physical phenomena involve no temporal dynamics, for example, a force applied to a spring, as noted earlier. Whether the force is the cause resulting in displacement of the spring or the other way around is an arbitrary choice. But in either case there must be a cause and an initiating time for any action. Thus, the idea of timelessness and there being no cause at all makes no sense in human language and cannot be understood as an argument for God.

JAMES'S VARIETIES OF RELIGIOUS EXPERIENCE

At the University of Edinburgh in 1901 and 1902, Harvard psychologist and philosopher William James presented the Gifford Lectures, published as *The Varieties of Religious Experience*.[8] The resulting book concerned the nature of religion and the neglect of science in the academic study of religion. Following its publication, the book entered the Western canon of psychology and philosophy, and has remained in print ever since. The lectures covered the following: religion and neurology, circumscription of the topic, the reality of the unseen, the religion of healthy-mindedness, the sick soul, the divided self and the process of its unification, conversion, saintliness, and mysticism. While James's language may be quaint in today's theology, it is interesting how a psychologist of that era talked about religion.

James criticized scientists for ignoring unseen aspects of the universe. Science studies some of reality but not all of it. James contended,

Vague impressions of something indefinable have no place in the rationalistic system. . . . If we look on one's whole mental life as it exists, we must confess that attempts to explain parts of it by rational means end up being relatively superficial. These parts can challenge you for proofs, attempt logic, and put you down with words.[9]

For James, saintliness includes the following:

1. A feeling of being in a wider life than that of this world's selfish little interests and a conviction . . . of the existence of an Ideal Power.
2. A sense of the friendly continuity of the ideal power with our own life and a willing self-surrender to its control.
3. An immense elation and freedom, as the outlines of the confining selfhood melt down.
4. A shifting of the emotional centre towards loving and harmonious affections, towards "yes, yes" and away from "no," where the claims of the nonego are concerned.

James identifies two main properties of a mystical experience:

1. Ineffability: "No adequate report of its contents can be given in words. . . . Its quality must be directly experienced; it cannot be imparted or transferred to others. . . . Mystical states are more like states of feeling than like states of intellect. No one can make clear to another who has never had a certain feeling, in what the quality or worth of it consists."
2. Noetic quality: "Although so similar to states of feeling, mystical states seem to those who experience them to be also states of knowledge. They are states of insight into depths of truth unplumbed by the discursive intellect. They are illuminations, revelations, full of significance and importance, all inarticulate though they remain; and as a rule they carry with them a curious sense of authority for after-time."[10]

He also identifies two subsidiary features that are often, but not always, found with mystical experiences:

1. Transiency: "Mystical states cannot be sustained for long."

2. Passivity: "The mystic feels as if his own will were in abeyance, and indeed sometimes as if he were grasped and held by a superior power."[11]

James was primarily interested in direct religious experiences. Theology and the organizational aspects of religion were of less interest. James finds that, "The only thing that [religious experience] unequivocally testifies to is that we can experience union with *something* larger than ourselves and in that union find our greatest peace."[12] He asserts that the higher power "should be both other and larger than our conscious selves."[13] He believed that religious experiences can have "morbid origins" in brain pathology and be irrational but nevertheless are largely positive. Unlike the bad ideas that people have under the influence of a high fever, after a religious experience the ideas and insights usually remain and are often valued for the rest of the person's life.

In the final chapter, James identifies a two-part "common nucleus" of all religions: (1) an uneasiness ("a sense that there is something wrong about us as we naturally stand") and (2) a solution ("a sense that we are saved from the wrongness by making proper connection with the higher powers"). James believed that the origins of a religion shed little light upon its value and a proposition of value (a judgment on "importance, meaning, or significance").

James saw "healthy-mindedness" as America's main contribution to religion. This is the religious experience of optimism and positive thinking, which James sees running from transcendentalists Emerson and Whitman to Mary Baker Eddy's Christian Science. At the extreme, the "healthy-minded" see sickness and evil as an illusion. James considered belief in the "mind cure" to be reasonable when compared to medicine as practiced at the beginning of the twentieth century. The "sick souls" ("morbid-mindedness"/the "twice-born") are merely those who hit bottom before their religious experience and those whose redemption gives relief from the pains they suffered beforehand. By contrast, the "healthy-minded" deny the need for such preparatory pain or suffering. James believes that "morbid-mindedness ranges over the wider scale of experience" and that while healthy-mindedness is a surprisingly effective "religious solution," "healthy-mindedness is inadequate as a philosophical doctrine." James describes the two types as being a mere matter of temperament: the healthy minded having a "constitutional incapacity for prolonged suffering" and the morbid-minded being prone to "religious mel-ancholia."[14]

TILLICH'S GROUND OF BEING

Theologian Paul Tillich (1886–1965) was concerned with human exis-tence, and in his *Systematic Theology* he discusses the "being" of human existence. He defines God as the transcendent "ground of being," that is, being itself, rather than a being per se (an object).[15] Others, for example, Kant, had tilted in the same direction, warning against an anthropological view of God. This is a difficult concept, for it can be taken to mean a creationist perspective that God made everything without himself/itself being anything. Tillich emphasized absolute faith. He used phrases like "God above God" to characterize his perspective and disparaged "theo-logical theism" of literal interpretation of the Bible. His critics assert that he was a pantheist or an atheist but not a Christian. The notion of a transcendent God is currently popular and has been celebrated by such writers as Karen Armstrong (see the "Opposing Perspectives" section). I further wrestle with "transcendent" later in the book.

THE FINE-TUNING OF COSMOLOGICAL PARAMETERS (ANTHROPIC PRINCIPLE)

From a scientist's perspective, this is perhaps the most credible argument for God's existence. The argument is that the parameters (physical con-stants) of the universe are fine-tuned and that if they varied from what they are by even some small percentage we would not exist. Are they really fine-tuned by God? Or are we just lucky? That all of the parameters would be as they are would seem highly improbable given all the other possibilities.

Physicist Martin Rees formulates the fine-tuning in terms of six di-mensionless constants:

N = ratio of the strength of gravity to that of electromagnetism
Epsilon (ε) = strength of the force binding nucleons into nuclei
Omega (ω) = relative importance of gravity and expansion energy in
   the Universe

Lambda (λ) = cosmological constant that appears in Einstein's theory
   of general relativity

Q = ratio of the gravitational energy required to pull a large galaxy
   apart to the energy equivalent of its mass

D = number of spatial dimensions in space-time[16]

Until recently this was a tough one for physics to explain. But recent theories of the universe shed light on this conundrum. There are many notions afloat that might provide answers, for instance, the statistical chance that our universe is simply one among many existing universes (and we happen to be lucky) or the notion that the big bang is just one stage of an infinitely long oscillation of new universes with differing parameters. We will further discuss the emerging multiverse theory in a later chapter.

NEAR-DEATH EXPERIENCES

A large number of people have written about their near-death experiences. After being in a coma and recovering, they describe seeing marvelous lights and colors, idyllic scenery, heavenly music, angels, and even communicating with Jesus or God. For example, one recent best seller written by a brain surgeon offers what he considers to be scientific proof that his vivid experience of being in heaven was not just a neurological artifact from his illness, but the real thing; however, the reader gets the distinct impression that the author has taken considerable poetic license. Furthermore, his description of his illness differs significantly from the reports in the press offered independently by the doctors who treated him. While most reports of near-death experiences have been debunked by investigators, there is no way to prove that these writers have not had the experiences they describe. These are private events not observable by others and cannot constitute reality based on the nominal requirements of science.

Part II

Knowledge, Science, and Modeling

4

ACQUIRING KNOWLEDGE

Physical concepts are free creatures of the human mind and are not, however it may seem, uniquely determined by the external world.—Albert Einstein, *Evolution of Physics*, 1938

Our belief in any particular natural law cannot have a safer basis than our unsuccessful critical attempts to refute it.—Karl Popper, *Conjectures and Refutations*, 1963

Nothing is easier than self-deceit. For what each man wishes, that he also believes to be true.—Demosthenes, 384 BC

Before turning to modern ideas about God it seemed fitting to interject a chapter on what the Enlightenment has brought: new emphasis on reason and the emergence of science—and what that implies in discussing God.

Being an academic who seeks to bridge psychology and technology, it seems only natural for me to base much of my religious perspective on the basic premises of science. Beyond that general professional conditioning, it seems to me that one cannot honestly embrace two kinds of belief in ultimate truth, one that is based on logic and science, as well as my own observations, and one that is based on traditional authoritarian ideas of an all-knowing, all-powerful, and all-loving God as "revealed" in biblical teaching. I see a conflict, and I can't have it both ways. As Richard Dawkins has stated, if scientific evidence of any of the "miracles" described in the Bible were ever observed in a credible way that would throw out much of what we now call science. [1]

This is not to say for a moment that metaphor, myth, art, and poetry, those aspects of being human that influence so much of our lives, whether we are scientists or not, are not admissible in our thinking and affecting our behavior. They are surely there. They constitute a piece of all of us, and we can only admit that they are mostly beyond the realm of science today. We are all spiritual beings (as best as we understand in our different ways what that word means). But being "spiritual" does not impose the requirement that we believe in a traditional omniscient, omnipotent, loving being that cares for each of us individually.

My own specialty within my technology/psychology field is modeling human-technology interaction.[2] I detail in this chapter what it means to model something, what a model assumes and does not assume, and why various thinkers have asserted that unless some thing or set of events can be credibly modeled in unambiguous denotative language one has no right to make claims about its existence or properties. For these reasons I provide this chapter on knowledge, science, and modeling, to paint in an essential background to how I think about God and my fellow humans.

There are many ways for humans to acquire knowledge. No doubt there are also many ways to classify the means to acquire knowledge. Here I mention just a few of them. Knowledge can be acquired by the brain during the evolutionary process by successive modifications to the genes. That finally results in fertilization of egg by sperm and the gestation process in the mother. Certainly, this depends on the biological "operating system" software that makes the brain, the sense organs, and the muscles work together. But evolution also plays at the level of higher cognitive function. As Noam Chomsky asserts, much of the syntactic structure of grammar is evidently built in at birth.[3] What knowledge we acquire after birth is a function of what we attend to, and what we attend to is a function of our motivation for allocating our attention, which ultimately is a function of what we know, so knowledge acquisition after birth is a causal circle.

Learning has to do with what sticks and how we respond to the stimuli we observe. One theory of learning is the process of Pavlovian (classical) conditioning, where a *conditioned stimulus*, originally neutral in its effect, becomes a signal that an inherently significant (reward or punishment) *unconditioned stimulus* is about to occur. This results only after multiple pairings, and the brain somehow remembers the association. The originally neutral stimulus becomes conditioned, meaning that the person (or animal) responds reflexively to the conditioned stimulus the same as she/he would to the unconditioned stimulus (e.g., the dog salivates with the light or bell).

Somewhat different is Skinnerian or *operant* conditioning.[4] This is where a voluntary random action (called a free operant) is rewarded (reinforced) and that association remembered, and after sufficient repetitions, the voluntary actions occur more often (if previously rewarded). Operant learning can be maintained even when rewards are infrequently paired with the conditioned action.

But there seems to be much more learning that is not conditioning of either type. Chomsky admitted to the lack of evidence that all language is acquired by conditioning. Knowledge can be public, where two or more people agree on some perception or interpretation, and others can access the same information. Or it can be private, where it has not or cannot be shared. The issue is tricky, and that is why modelability is proposed as a criterion for what can be called public knowledge. Two people can look at what we call a red rose and agree that it is red because they have been conditioned to respond with the word "red" upon observing that stimulus. But ultimately, exactly what they experienced cannot be shared.

We can posit that some learning is simply accepting, unquestioningly, information from some source because that source is trusted or because the learner is compelled in some way to learn. (This is probably how many professed believers in God acquired their belief.) We finally contrast the aforementioned models to learning by means of the scientific method, which is detailed here: Critical observation and hypothesizing are followed by collection of evidence, analysis, logical conclusions, and modeling to serve one's own use or communicate to others.

WHAT IS THE SCIENTIFIC METHOD

Science has its own formal model of how to determine the truth. The scientific method is usually stated as consisting of the following nine steps:

1. Gather information and resources (informal observation).

2. Question the relationships between aspects of some objects or events, based on observation and contemplation. An incipient mental model may already form in the observer's head.

3. Hypothesize a conjecture resulting from the act of questioning. This can be either a predictive or explanatory hypothesis. In either case it should be stated explicitly in terms of independent and dependent variables (causes and effects).

4. Predict the logical consequences of the hypothesis. (A model will begin to take shape.)

5. Test the hypothesis by doing formal data collection and experiments to determine whether the world behaves according to the prediction. This includes taking pains to design the data-taking and the experiment to minimize risks of experimental error. It is crucial that the tests be recorded in enough detail so as to be observable and repeatable by others. The experimental design will have a large effect on what model might emerge.

6. Analyze the results of the experiment and draw tentative conclusions. This often involves a secondary hypothesis step, namely exercising the statistical null hypothesis. The null hypothesis is that some conjecture about a population of related objects or events is false, namely, that observed differences have occurred by chance, for example, that some disease is not affected by some drug. Normally the effort is to show a degree of statistical confidence in the failure and thus the rejection of the null hypothesis. In other words, if there is enough confidence that the differences did not occur by chance, then the conjectured relationship exists.

7. Draw formal conclusions and model as appropriate.

8. Communicate the results, conclusions, and model to colleagues in publication or verbal presentation, rendering the model in a form that best summarizes and communicates the determined relationships.

9. Retest and refine the model (frequently done based on review and critique by other scientists).

OBSERVATIONS ON THE SCIENTIFIC METHOD

This is also called the hypothetico-deductive method. As stated, it is an idealization of the way science really works, as the aforementioned steps are seldom cleanly separated, and the process is typically messy. Oftentimes experimentation is done to make observations that provoke additional observations, questions, hypotheses, predictions, and rejections or refinements of the starting hypothesis. Especially at the early observation stage the process can be very informal. One of my students used to say that what we did in the lab was "piddling with a purpose." Einstein is said to have remarked that the most important tool of the scientist is the wastebasket.

Francis Bacon (1620) asserted that observations must be collected "without prejudice."[5] But as scientists are real people, there is no way they can operate free of some prejudice. They start with some bias as to their initial knowledge and interests, social status and physical location, and available tools of observation. They are initially prejudiced as to what is of interest, what observations are made, and what questions are asked.

Philosopher Karl Popper (1934) believed that all science begins with a prejudiced hypothesis.[6] He further asserted that actually a theory can never be proven correct by observation, but can only be proven incorrect by disagreement with observation. Scientific method is about falsifiability. That is the basis of the null hypothesis test in statistics mentioned earlier. (But, of course, the falsifiability is itself subject to statistical error; one can only reject the null hypothesis with some small chance of being wrong.) The American Association for the Advancement of Science asserted in a legal brief to the U.S. Supreme Court (1993) that, "Science is not an encyclopedic body of knowledge about the universe. Instead, it represents a *process* for proposing and refining theoretical explanations about the world that are subject to further testing and refinement."[7]

Historian Thomas Kuhn (1970) offered a different perspective on how science works, namely, in terms of *paradigm shifts*.[8] Whether in psychology or cosmology, researchers seem to make small and gradual refinements of accepted models, until new evidence and an accompanying model provokes a radical shift in paradigm, to which scientists then adhere for a time. When a new paradigm is in the process of emerging the competition between models and their proponents can be fierce, even personal (who discovered X first, who published first, whose model offers the best explanation). We also must admit that the search for truth is not the only thing that motivates us as scientists and modelers. We are driven by ambition for recognition from our peers, as well as money.

I emphasize again the relevance of reproducible observability. Having to deal with observables is the most crucial factor in an epistemological sense (what we know). This is because it distinguishes what may be called truth based on scientific evidence that is openly observable from experiences that are not observable by others (e.g., personal testimony and anecdotal evidence). Observability also comes into play for what are called mental models.

Mental representations (*mental models*), being private, are not subject to direct observation by other people. Experiments in psychophysics, where subjects make verbal category judgments or button-push responses to physical stimuli of sound, light, etc., are regarded as conforming to scientific method. This is because the human is making a direct mechanical response to a given stimulus, for instance, pushing a button, not having to articulate in arbitrary words what he or she is thinking; however, when subjects are asked to explicate in their own words their mental models of how they believe something works or the cognitive steps of a particular task as might be asked, there is no physical reference. Here scientific method is more challenging. Credibility demands that there be repeatability or aggregation of the results from many subjects. Observability clearly is a challenge for modeling what God is, although not as much for modeling human behavior in the practice of religion.

While social scientists often point out that humans have a predilection for reaffirming the status quo, science nevertheless is a truth system committed to change, as warranted, rather than preservation. But while science actively pursues possibilities of change, the null hypothesis testing, by its very nature, demands a significant level of statistical confidence to reject the null hypothesis that there is no real change (that there is only random difference between the hypothesized variant and the control).

The scientific method is a procedure wherein inquiry regards itself as fallible and purposely probes, criticizes, corrects, and improves itself. This universally accepted attribute stands in sharp contrast to religious traditions throughout the world. Science is the one human endeavor that has proven relatively immune to the passions that otherwise divide us.

LOGICAL REASONING

A representation of a thing or event (i.e., a model) may be derived from logical reasoning, or it may be stated out of ignorance or for purposes of deception. It may also be a metaphorical model, where, because of ambiguity in the words or drawings, it is not possible to conclude that it is logical. If it is based on logic and assuming no ambiguity in the words, pictures, or symbols, it is relevant to mention three different types of logical reasoning:

Deduction allows deriving *b* from *a* only where *b* is a formal logical consequence of *a*. In other words, deduction is the process of deriving the consequences of what is assumed. Given the truth of the assumptions, a valid deduction guarantees the truth of the conclusion. For example, given that all bachelors are unmarried males, and given that some person is a bachelor, it can be deduced that the person in question is an unmarried male.

Induction allows inferring *b* from *a*, where *b* does not follow necessarily from *a*. *A* might give us very good reason to accept *b*, but it does not ensure that *b* is true. For example, if all of the swans that we have observed so far are white, we may induce that all swans are white. We have good reason to believe the conclusion from the premise, but the truth of the conclusion is not guaranteed. (Indeed, it turns out that some swans are black.)

Abduction allows inferring *a* as an explanation of *b*. Put another way, abduction allows the precondition *a* to be abduced from the consequence *b*. Deduction and abduction thus differ in the direction in which a rule like "*a entails b*" is used for inference. As such abduction is formally equivalent to a logical fallacy, that a unique *a* occurs where there are multiple possible explanations for *b*. For example, after glancing up and seeing the eight ball moving in some direction, we may abduce that it was struck by the cue ball. The cue ball's strike would account for the eight ball's movement. It serves as a hypothesis that explains our observation. There are, in fact, many possible explanations for the eight ball's movement, and so our abduction does not leave us certain that the cue ball did in fact strike the eight ball, but our abduction is still useful and can serve to orient us in our surroundings. This process of abduction is an instance of the scientific method. Logically there are infinite possible explanations for any of the physical processes we observe, but from our experience we are inclined to abduce a single explanation (or a few explanations) for them in the hopes that we can better orient ourselves in our surroundings and then eliminate some of the possibilities.[9]

PRIVATE (SUBJECTIVE) AND PUBLIC (OBJECTIVE) KNOWLEDGE

Representation of a thing or event necessarily begins in the head of some person, and only later is it rendered in words, graphics, or mathematical language so that it can be communicated to others. As previously noted, the term "mental model" refers broadly to a person's private thoughts. Some psychologists would confine the use of that term to well-formed ideas about the structure or function of some objects or events, such that it is potentially communicable in understandable format to another person.

For many years, psychologists have struggled with how to extract a person's mental model. Psychophysical methods of having experimental subjects rank-order stimuli or assign preferential numbers or descriptive categories (as done by political pollsters) is a common approach. With more complex situations, and particularly those that have social implications, a problem is that what people say they believe and what they actually believe may be quite different. People are inclined to say what they think some other person wants to hear; social etiquette reinforces this behavior. (Many churchgoers would fall into this category when professing their religious beliefs.)

DOUBT AND ITS RELATION TO DOING SCIENCE

Many philosophers, from René Descartes[10] to Charles Sanders Peirce,[11] have proposed methodological doubting (also called Cartesian skepticism, methodological skepticism, or hyperbolic doubt) as a means to test the truth of one's beliefs. Descartes applied the method to doubting his own existence, leading to a "proof," namely, *Cogito ergo sum* (I think, therefore I am). If he was able to doubt, he must be alive and real. I recall attending a "Skeptics Seminar" at MIT, at which the famous mathematician and founder of cybernetics, Norbert Wiener, emphasized the importance of doubting to refine one's beliefs.

Doubt is deliberation on error and failure. Together with a graduate student I once offered an experimental graduate course called "Seminar on Failure," in which historians, psychiatrists, scientists, and engineers were invited to reminisce on failures in their own professional experiences. We learned that error and failure often led to discovery and learning, and that success often led to overconfidence, carelessness, and eventually failure. Failure and success are the Taoist yin and yang of our experience; they are mutually complementary; one could not exist without the other.

Doubt and questioning motivate scientists to think of different hypotheses and try different experiments. A pioneer in cybernetics, Ross Ashby (1903–1972) is known for his "law of requisite variety," which asserts that for one system to control another it must possess the ability to engage a greater variety of states.[12] This "law" has been applied to genetic mutations believed to be essential to the evolution of species, as per Darwin's theory. There is requisite variety in our own social and environmental encounters in life, from which we can refine our actions and resulting beliefs for what works and what does not work. Edwin Hubble's doubt and resulting tests led to the discovery that the brightness of a spot in the Andromeda cluster could not have come from our own galaxy, the first proof that there were other galaxies in the universe.[13] Sometimes it is not simply doubt, but absolute failure, that provokes a wider search for solution and improvement, whether in a computer or a person.

USING AND AVOIDING EVIDENCE

Thus far the discussion has assumed that a rational person accepts a model or a belief because the preponderance of evidence supports that model or belief. People are always free to "choose" a belief because it is what parents or peers say they believe or what individuals believe they should believe, for whatever reason. Perhaps it is because they think believing will make them feel better or there will be punishment for professing disbelief or even considering disbelief. But these are not acts of seeking truth. No one says that truth-seeking is easy, particularly when what appears to be the rational truth is in conflict with claims by authority figures or other trusted sources.

Let's face it, truth-seeking has its costs. In many ways, evolution has designed us not to be rational in every act. Hyperrational insistence on barefaced truth clearly gets us into trouble—in interpersonal relations where etiquette is required, in supporting and defending a child from destructive criticism, in winning an argument, etc. The truth may be messy and ugly. Some will surely feel that absolute truth is second to happiness, and who will ever know the ultimate truth anyway? Isn't happiness the real goal? In any case, we may want to be careful about flaunting what we believe to be the truth.

METAPHYSICS AND ITS RELATION TO SCIENCE

Metaphysics is a traditional branch of philosophy concerned with being—what things exist and what are their properties. Prior to the eighteenth century all questions of ultimate reality were addressed by philosophers. Aristotle believed that things have within them their own purpose (a teleology).[14] He is well known for distinguishing between two essential properties of things: *potentiality* (the possibility of any property a thing can have) and *actuality* (what is actually in evidence). There are modern manifestations of Aristotle's dichotomy, for example, the distinction between potential and kinetic energy in physics. Thomas Aquinas called metaphysics the "queen of sciences" and wrote widely on the subject.

Since the Enlightenment the field of metaphysics has evolved into a philosophical pursuit of topics that have not been easy for science to handle, for instance, religion, being (existence), mind, perception, free will, consciousness, and meaning. In later sections of the book we will discuss how science has begun to confront some of these issues. Whether throughout time they will be clarified or remain as conundrums, or whether the verbal constructs will just fade away, remains to be determined. I would guess some of each.

As noted earlier, Descartes's conclusion that, "I think, therefore I am," was proffered as a metaphysical basis for his own existence. He asserted that while all else could be doubted, the fact that he could do the doubting meant that he must exist to doubt. Such thought experiments are common in philosophy. Recall the thought experiment rationale offered by Anselm of Canterbury, that to imagine a thing or event is to make it exist, namely, his famous "proof of God."[15] Surely thoughts exist as neural activity in the brains of people who have the thoughts; they constitute what we have called mental models. But our concern here is for existence of things perceived from observables, other than as one person's imagination.

OBJECTIVITY, ADVOCACY, AND BIAS

Ideally the scientist is supposed to be disinterested in and completely impartial to how any test of a hypothesis turns out, and what the implications of the results are to the world. But scientists are people, and people do things because they are interested in achieving some objectives. The very act of formulating a hypothesis is a creative act, motivated by the interests of the scientist. But given this unavoidable level of interest, the scientist has an obligation to be as objective as possible and not favor one aspect of the results while hiding some other aspect. This is an unavoidable imperfection of human nature and puts a constraint on any effort at denotative language.

For example, everyone is subject to bias, including this author. Psychologists have studied human biases extensively. In dealing with such value-laden topics as religion biases are especially salient. One most pertinent category of bias is what is called the *confirmation bias*. Psychologist Raymond Nickerson defines the confirmation bias as the "seeking or interpreting of evidence in ways that are partial to existing beliefs, expectations, or a hypothesis in hand."[16] He reviews evidence of such a bias in a variety of guises and gives examples of its operation in several practical contexts. Other biases include overconfidence in one's own predictions, giving more weight to recent events as compared to earlier events in judging probabilities, assessing greater risk to situations one is forced into as compared to those voluntarily selected, and inferring illusory causal relations.

Many democratic societies have judicial systems based on advocacy, where the advocates of the two or more sides of any argument confront one another in a highly procedural venue in front of a jury of peers. The assumption is that the jury can judge the arguments, weigh the evidence presented, and detect efforts to hide something. Because conventional jury selection is not set up to include experts on particular fields of science or technology, there have been various proposals to develop "science courts" that would somehow demand more rigorous objectivity in presenting and judging arguments and evidence. (One can only imagine the difficulty the U.S. Supreme Court has in confronting the evidence in regard to challenges based on religious belief.)

ANALOGY AND METAPHOR

Analogy is a broad class of cognitive process or linguistic expression involving the transfer of meaning from one object or event to another because of some similarity. Analogy plays a crucial role in creativity, problem-solving, memory, perception, explanation, and communication. It can also be said that science depends on metaphor (and simile) in the sense that an active and curious observer is constantly seeing analogies, likenesses between elements of nature. The observed likenesses lead to hypotheses that permit generalization.

For example, in the field of physics, mechanical force, mechanical pressure, electrical voltage, and temperature are all seen as having the property of effort. Mechanical velocity, fluid flow, electrical current, and heat flow are seen as having the property of flow. Mechanical friction, fluid viscosity, electrical resistance, and thermal insulation have the property of resistance to flow. Depending on the spatial configuration the differential equations relating the forces, flows, and resistance to flow are identical. These analogies are powerful concepts in physical science that also have counterparts in traffic analysis, economics, and other fields. Much academic teaching in the physical sciences and engineering employs analogy.

A metaphor is a figure of speech that makes use of analogy. It is a word or phrase describing a thing or action that is regarded as representative or symbolic of something else, especially something abstract—even though it is not literally applicable. This is in contrast to a simile, in which something is said to be *like* something else and the attribute of likeness is spelled out or implied. Joseph Campbell (1904–1987) uses the following examples: The boy *runs like* a deer (simile). The boy *is* a deer (metaphor).[17]

Literature, poetry, music, and the arts are full of metaphor; they depend on metaphor. Metaphor can say things more emotionally powerful than simple rational statements. Metaphor provokes the human imagination, as in myths, allegories, and parables. It has been said that literature and the arts often realize human truths well before other branches of human endeavor do. Since it is a figure of speech, a metaphor is not a belief (a mental event); rather, it is a way to describe a belief. Things are not metaphors, but they can be expressed through metaphors. Every metaphor is both metaphorically true (if it is an apt description) and literally false.

An analog representation, whether in words or any other medium, can be a model. This author cut his academic teeth using analog computers as models of human behavior. The point is that certain relationships (e.g., in magnitude and time of the graphical traces output by the analog computer) *denote* magnitude and time relationships of the target thing or events being modeled. It is understood by the user of the analog computer that other properties of the analog computer (physical hardware, electron flow) are irrelevant.

Metaphorical description can be a kind of model, although not a scientific model, as previously noted. This is because the interpretation of the metaphor as a representation of the target object or event is a creative act by the reader or listener, since the connection between the metaphor and the target is not explicit (it is *connotative*). Religious myth fits this category.

5

MODELING, A CRITERION OF KNOWING

While not disputing that all sentient humans have feelings of love, appreciation of beauty, and awe in nature and the universe, atheists question whether these feelings fall short of a basis for asserting that God exists—at least the traditional all-knowing, all-powerful, all-loving kind of God. Atheists also understand the natural longing people experience for some kind of "father figure," a benevolent authority or force that can make us all healthy and happy. A question raised by this book is whether thoughts about what God *is*, while expressible in the connotative language of myth, can be sufficiently described in the terms of science—in other words, modeled denotatively.

DEFINITION OF "MODEL"

What do a verbal treatise on how some aspect of the economy works, a miniature replica of an airplane, a mathematical equation characterizing driver steering behavior, and a girl posing for a camera or painter have in common? We call each of them a model. There are other entities that we normally do not call models, for instance, a myth or poem, but by a broad definition they too are models, although not the kind this book focuses on.

Various authors, including physicist Stephen Hawking, have asserted that if some thing or event cannot be modeled in what we are calling denotative or scientific language, we have no right to claim that we "know" it.[1] For purposes of this book a model is defined as a concise, denotative representation of the structure or function of some selected aspects of our world to one or more observers for the purposes of communicating a belief about some relationships, expressing a conjecture, making a prediction, or specifying a design of a thing or a set of events.

Obviously, the term "model" as defined here is quite general. Beyond the idea of *representation* are such synonyms as specification, rendering, map, or characterization of the relations between elements or variables of the defined set of objects or events. There are semantic overlaps with related terms like abstraction, construction, explanation, portrayal, depiction, theory, idea, concept, paradigm, pattern, etc.

An important word in the above definition is *selected*. No model purports to include all of the factors (variables) relating to the target object or set of events. Much (indeed most) will be left out. It is obligatory that the modeler specify which variables are included, and by implication everything else is omitted. The idea is to capture the independent variables that have the greatest effect on the dependent variables of interest.

A model can be said to be a description of a concept. Models can be described using words, graphics (e.g., graphs, diagrams, pictures), mathematical equations, physical things, or some combination of these (e.g., computer simulations that run equations and output numbers, graphs, dynamic animations, etc.). The word "concise" is added to the aforementioned definition to emphasize that a model states the intended relationships briefly but completely and unambiguously, eliminating redundancy and extraneous words or symbols. This excludes long-winded, wordy statements or graphics with elaboration that are unnecessary to the message. Unfortunately, there is no clean distinction as to when a particular statement qualifies as a model.

Semiotics is the theory of signs, which includes *syntax* (grammar, structural constraints of words or symbols), *semantics* (their meaning), and *pragmatics* (effects of their use on people). Semiotics makes an important distinction between *denotation* and *connotation*. Denotation refers to the explicit literal meaning of the words, symbols, or signs. Connotation refers to the implied or suggested meaning, as with metaphor. A photo of or a verbal statement about a red rose with a green stem *denotes* nothing more than a red rose with a green stem, but it *connotes* affection or celebration. In this book we mostly restrict the word "model" to denotative representation. This accords with the use of models in every field of science.

Modern society makes ever-greater use of denotative models, particularly in science and technology. Dating from early Greek civilization we have had verbal models, but more and more since the Enlightenment we have seen the development of mathematical, graphical, and other symbolic models. Our ability to run fast-time computer simulations on large databases for weather, physics, engineering, economics, genomics, transportation, etc., has made huge strides in recent years.

A model typically states explicitly, or at least strongly implies, an "IF X, THEN Y" relationship. For example, if you look at a particular location X on a map or within the human body, you will find Y. Or, if X is the input or independent variable to a given system or process, then Y will be the result. The latter is common to a scientific model that is intended to generalize about and predict observations.

Mostly scientific models are intended to be predictive so as to be useful in some application. It can be said that models without application are useless (essentially by definition if "application" is interpreted broadly). It should be noted that basic science routinely develops models that are used only to communicate understanding of how the world works, which only much later may find practical application.

Some people distinguish a model from a theory, where a model is a rendering of specific relationships relevant to a theory, a theory being a statement that circumscribes some relationships within the larger, more complex reality. The theory can be just a hypothesis, or it can be an accepted statement of some reality. Ideally the theory includes statements of constraints on application: where, when, and how the theory or the derived model applies or does not apply. So models and theories of application naturally go together, and unfortunately the terms are often used to mean the same thing.

Random examples of denotative models in different applications might be as follows:

Business model: a framework of the business logic of a firm
Computer model: a computer program that simulates abstractions
about a particular system
Ecosystem model: a representation of components and flows through
an ecosystem

Physiological response model: a description of a neural process that
   simulates the response of the motor system to estimate the outcome
   of a neural command

Macroeconomic model: a representation of some aspect of a national
   or regional economy

Map: used for navigation by air, sea, or land

Mechanism model: a description of a system in terms of its constituent
   parts and mechanisms

Molecular model: a physicochemical or symbolic description of the
   behavior of molecules

Pension model: a description of a pension system, including simulations and projections of assets

Standard model of physics: the theory in particle physics that describes certain fundamental forces and particles

Statistical model: in applied statistics, a parameterized set of probability distributions

Wiring diagram: as used by an electrician

It is important to note that models of cognition, what people think and
believe, are generated from observable data of what human subjects say
or do in controlled laboratory experiments, where subject responses are
not expressed in free form, but are highly constrained so that credible
averages and statistics may be calculated by aggregating subject responses.

ATTRIBUTES OF A MODEL

It is useful to think of the value of a model in terms of its component
properties, its attributes. These are as follows:

Applicability to observables. *Observables* here refers to objects or
   events that can be sensed directly by humans or measured using
   some repeatable physical means. And it is important to note that
   the objects or events must potentially be observable by *any* human;
   personal experiences that cannot be shared with others do not count
   as observables, a criterion well established in the philosophy of
   science.

Dimensionality. *Dimensionality* refers to the number of dimensions of the independent (input, or cause) and dependent (output, or effect) variable states: how many input and output variables are in the model. A model can be single-input-single-output, multi-input-single-output, or multi-input-multi-output. Single-input-multi-output makes sense only insofar as the outputs are understood to be 100 percent correlated (if the model is deterministic) and thus constitutes only a single complex output. The world is complicated, and in general, a complex of many outputs (a vector) is a complex function of many inputs (another vector). Some such input variables may be known, while their effects are unknown. In contrast there are the unknown-unknowns, variables that the modeler is not even aware of (so-called "unk-unks").

Metricity. *Metricity* (the quality, or degree of the sophistication of what the numbers mean) has to do with the well-known psychophysical measurement scales of S. S. Stevens.[2] At one extreme are numbers that are only name identifiers (e.g., social security numbers, just arbitrarily different for different people or things). Next are measures in terms of their rank order (Y is greater than X). More sophisticated are measures of linear differences (Y = X + K), and finally come ratios (Y = X times K).

Robustness. *Robustness* refers to the breadth of applicability. The least robust model is one that has only one purpose, a unique application, and is otherwise useless. An example might be an instruction for how to operate a particular home appliance or item of software. At the other extreme is a model that has very wide applicability, say Newton's law, F = MA, i.e., force equals mass times acceleration. We can assert that in the limit a model that applies to everything from atomic scale to galactic scale does not exist, although physicists are now thinking hard about what it would take for a "theory of everything."

Social penetration. *Social penetration* has to do with the degree to which a model is known, understood, accepted, and used by the appropriate community of people. The scale goes from purely mental models that are confined to internal thoughts of some one person, to models that are widely understood, accepted, and applied by a large and diverse community of people. In between are models that are described to others or published in the literature, perhaps in

competition with other models for the same application, and perhaps used by only a few practitioners.

Conciseness. *Conciseness* is added to the taxonomy to provide a metric for brevity of presentation, along with adherence to denotation,
clarity, and reason. Adherence to brevity, denotation, clarity, and
reason is the principle that has come to be called *Ockham's razor*.
This principle was originally attributed to philosopher William of
Ockham (1288–1347), according to his pronouncement *Numquam
ponenda est pluralitas sine necessitate* (Plurality must never be
posited without necessity).[3] The idea is that one should use the
simplest statement that does not compromise explanatory power.
Of course, too few words may reduce explanatory power. A hun-
dred-page exposition of an argument, theory, premise, or relationship would not normally be considered as a model. This book is not
a model, although this taxonomy of model attributes is a model.[4]

These six attributes are continuous over a range from none to "high
level." While it may seem that the explicit prediction (for a given input
what is the output) is the most useful property of a model, that is often of
only secondary importance. The most useful aspect may well be that the
conception, development, and publication of the model caused people to
think hard about the problem—what are the variables that count the most,
how best to formulate the problem, and so on. A model requires the
model-builder to think, and it should also require the model-reader/mod-
el-user to think, and more thinking is usually a good thing.

From a scientific perspective, the totality of our publicly accepted
models forms our store of what we reasonably assume we know. Individual mental models encapsulate individual subjective beliefs, whether
based on evidence or faith, but they do not contribute to the general store
of knowledge—they are private. Unfortunately, at this point in our evolution we mostly lack objective means to capture individual mental models
and somehow compare them or combine them where they agree. People
can share mental models by verbal expression or by acting on their beliefs, as in coordinated athletic team sports, where individuals infer each
other's mental models as they interact.

One objective means to discover a mental model is using voting to
capture the mental preferences or beliefs of a group. Pollsters work hard
in posing simple questions to get valid answers about what people really
believe. The problem here is that the simple questions are posed in words

that often have ambiguous interpretation: Do you believe in X? What kind of X? Do people all mean the same thing by what is being called X? What does "believe" mean? Do I believe X or not believe X because that is my tradition, or because that is what is comfortable for me to say I believe? Did I really ever question my belief in X? For religious belief, especially because of its subtleties, it is difficult to pin down by polling what people actually believe.

IMPORTANT DISTINCTIONS IN MODELING

Beyond the six model attributes detailed earlier in this chapter there are several other modeling distinctions that are important to consider.

Simple and complex models. A simplest model is a statement that X is Y, where X is a thing or event and Y is a descriptor (adjective, number, etc.). A very complex model might be the complete engineering specification of a jumbo jet aircraft or the voluminous U.S. Code of Federal Regulations. In the simplest model case, the independent variables have to do with what qualifies as X. For the jumbo jet the independent variables have to do with what exact part of the airplane, and what function of that part, we are talking about. For the Code of Federal Regulations, the independent variables would provide information enabling a user to go to a specific chapter and rule, and determine what the regulation stated. Some readers might complain that I am using the term "model" too broadly here, but there is really no way to restrict the term to a narrower range.

Descriptive and prescriptive models. A *descriptive* model serves to tell how some specific thing is structured or provide detail on some set of events. It looks back in time in the sense that it refers to objects or events that exist or have existed in the past. If the model describes an object yet to be built or a plan yet to be implemented, the descriptive model is based on the already completed design or plan. A *prescriptive* or *normative* model tells what *should* happen in the future according to specified or assumed norms. They can be social/cultural norms, or they can be physical norms, for example, how some aspect of the world works: that a (given) input should produce a stated output.

Static and dynamic models. In a *static* model neither the input nor the output variables change with time, while in a *dynamic* model either input or output, or both, vary with time. For example, when you press down with force F on a spring having stiffness parameter K, it will deflect a certain distance X. That is a static model; nothing changes with time. If a clock pendulum is initially displaced from a resting position to angle A and then released, a simple dynamic model will predict the trajectory of how it will swing back and forth with time as a function of initial angle A, the pendulum length and the force of gravity. An economic dynamic model might have as input the continually changing price of gasoline during a one-year period, and as output the modeled effect of those changes on vehicle use during the same period. Static models require only algebraic equations, whereas dynamic models make use of differential equations with time as the argument. Thus, the output of a dynamic model is a curve that plots one or more variables against time. Whether the model is static or dynamic, a computer can be programmed to try a large number of different inputs to test the resulting outputs. The inputs can systematically proceed by intervals through a given range of values or be selected randomly from a given distribution. The latter is called a Monte Carlo model, after the casino-gambling reputation of the Principality of Monaco.

Deterministic and probabilistic models. A *deterministic* model says that if X is the input, then Y is the output—for certain. A *probabilistic* model says that if X is the input, then Y is the output, with some probability less than one. More generally, for input X, the probabilistic model will specify a set of outputs, each with a different probability (possibly a smooth probability distribution). A common type of probabilistic model (called a Markov model) is a tree graph that branches from one or more nodes representing initial states, where the branches to downstream or peripheral nodes are tagged with probabilities. Starting from any initial node the probabilities of ending in any downstream node is thus calculable.

Models that use fuzzy logic. In recent years a new analytical tool has found increasing acceptance as a way to represent the "soft associations" exhibited by the overlaps of meaning between words. It is called *fuzzy logic* or *fuzzy set theory*. It has applicability to making decisions involving a large number of variables where the many rules available for deciding on an action in any specific context are only available as verbal statements (which is the case for the explication of most real knowledge in this world). Fuzzy logic has a fascinating history of rejection by computer scientists in the West, even though *crisp* mathematical ways of thinking have proven ineffectual in dealing with soft, overlapping ideas. Technology managers are often put off by the term "fuzzy" as being unscientific. At the same time, theorists in Asia have pushed ahead with not only fuzzy theory, but also applications. Systems based on fuzzy logic are now in digital cameras, washing machines, subway speed controls, and automobile transmissions.[5]

6

CAN GOD OR RELIGION BE MODELED?

CAN THE NATURE OF GOD BE MODELED?

Concise, explicit (denotative) models based on observable objects or events is the way of science, and it is a proven discipline for thinking, and for making knowledge public. Yet, connotative language, including myth and metaphor, provides another way of depicting belief. Such belief is surely life-enriching, although the reader's interpretation in the latter case is arbitrary, open-ended, and not publicly verifiable. One can try to share how one *feels* about something, but the basis for the feeling is ultimately private.

When modeling human belief there can be a model of the nature of an object or set of events that people believe to be real, or there can be a model of the reasons or process or mechanism of acquiring and practicing such a belief. Modeling God per se is of the first sort. In this case the modeler asks, "What *is* God?"—that is, what is the structure and function of God? How to represent the phenomenon, nature, attributes, or character of God? What can God do? And how and in what circumstances?

Can current ideas about the nature of God be evaluated on the basis of the taxonomy of attributes presented here? Can means of representation (verbal, graphic, or logical symbolism, including mathematics) be used? Consider how each of the six attributes might apply, where the assertion was that to the degree that these attributes are present in the fullest sense, we have a model that represents true and useful knowledge. Let's see how well they apply to God.

Applicability to observables. If any and all of creation can be called observable, then we are stuck with the question of what is God *not*? There are no data on God, or else the data set includes every-thing—all of creation. There is nothing that can be observed in any public operational way to distinguish God from anything else. Pri-vate transcendental feelings are not operational, and so there is nothing to observe.

Dimensionality. Swinburne asserts that God is the ultimate in simplic-ity (one dimension—or none). But what exactly is that? Others would claim that God would have to have at least as many dimen-sions as whatever He creates, which is infinity. That would be impossible to model by any standard of human capability.

Metricity. In a pantheistic physical universe God would have to com-ply with criteria of physics and support a cardinal (ratio) metric in every one of His (infinite) dimensions. Again, this is impossible to model, so we still have no measurable basis for a model.

Robustness. What is God good for? What can He do? He can make you feel good if you are a believer. And if you believe in revealed truth as in the sacred texts, He can serve as a supposed basis for morality and a motivation for good works. He can also serve as a basis for hate and for fighting religious wars that we have wit-nessed throughout history and which continue to this day. The construct of God is robust for sure—one might say infinitely ro-bust. God is a good rationale for just about everything—many would say rationalization. How do we come to agreement of what use to make of the God idea?

Social penetration. Here the God construct excels. The concept has penetrated the culture for thousands of years with wide acceptance. No arguments otherwise.

Conciseness. I just wish the theist philosophers who defend the exis-tence of God could be concise in their arguments. I find them circular and very confusing. In contrast, there are the oft-repeated descriptors: omniscient, omnipotent, and omnibenevolent—con-cise for sure but hardly constituting an acceptable model beyond the mental model of active imagination. (I can imagine that my pink unicorn example has those same attributes.)

So the God construct flatly fails the first three criteria (no trace of an observable God, the dimensionality would have to be zero or infinite and therefore unworkable, and no basis for a metric). The God construct surely is robust in the sense that one can try to apply it to anything. In applicability the minuses seem just as great as the plusses (suffering versus happiness). With regard to robustness, in terms of credibility, it was mathematician Pierre-Simon Laplace (1749–1827) who famously said, "I have no need for that hypothesis," when he was referring to God in relation to celestial mechanics. For social penetration, God surely is a winner: The concept has thoroughly pervaded history. Of course, the belief that the world was flat did quite well on the social penetration scale. As to conciseness, if one is happy with "omnipotent, omniscient, and omnibenevolent," that's pretty concise.

In any case, God can be said to be a private mental model, something imagined, an idea, however vague the explanation. So God (and a god) is a robust, pervasive *connotative idea* that can be used by anyone for almost any purpose, and has been for thousands of years. In all other respects, there is nothing there to model, certainly not by the standards of modeling in science.

WHAT IS THERE TO MODEL ABOUT GOD?

The modeling approaches previously discussed require some input data, something observable to the modeler that can be reported as data. Unfortunately, as readily acknowledged by theist scholars, observables are totally lacking. Philosopher Meister Eckhart (1260–1327) said it many years ago: "God is no thing," meaning not a tangible object.[1] In contrast to God being no thing, God has been said to be everything, infinity, all of creation. Mathematicians and philosophers have been struggling to cope with zero and infinity for a long time.

Modeling infinity is no different from modeling zero with respect to discriminating observables. There is no way to make any distinctions. Zero and infinity are defined as mathematical limits. They are useful concepts in mathematics, fitting into mathematical models, mostly as ways of saying what cannot be modeled. By themselves, zero and infinity do not constitute models of anything.

Theists agree that God has no space or time dimension. That proscribes any model of physical objects or events by any human being who lives in a world confined to space and time. And that necessarily makes

God an idea, a meme, something imagined, a mental model. As noted earlier, at least in Abrahamic religions, God has been depicted as an old man sitting on a throne in the sky, surrounded by angels with harps. These *images* have been modeled, for example, as pictures on ceilings or stained-glass windows of churches. But today few would accept these images as accurate models of God in the sense the term "model" has been used here. We can also use objective methods to get people to describe what God means to them and collect data on their verbal or graphical responses, but there would be little consistency. In any case, insofar as God exists for different individuals as private, imagined, mental representations, we are obliged to exclude these from what we have called denotative or scientific models that can be communicated and applied publicly.

However, there is one caveat. Insofar as God is represented by physical events in the brain, there truly *are* observables potentially available. Just now they are difficult to measure. Neuroscientists may someday correlate those brain events with other events in the body or the external world. Not much is promising at the moment.

It is fashionable nowadays to say that God is *transcendent,* but the meaning of that word is difficult to get one's arms around. There is no consensus on the meaning of transcendent. Modeling a transcendent entity seems out of the question, except perhaps by such descriptors of God as power, knowledge, love, or beauty—or God as an ultimate hidden and mysterious force behind everything. By themselves those are metaphorical terms, or they might be called attributes of a metaphorical model. But such a representation does not pass the crucial observability criterion of a scientific model.

Getting a person to make a selection as to the most fitting verbal phrase in a questionnaire, as is done by pollsters, does create observables. But because the pollster is the one who constructed the questionnaire, that provides questionable meaning with respect to a scientific model of the individual subject's idea of God. And polling of such data shades into what is discussed in the next section as measuring behavior of people's practice of worship, that is, modeling the behavior of religious people (in contrast to modeling God per se).

Some people have asserted that our relationship to God is similar to an emotional relationship with another person. A religious person loves, honors, and glorifies God, but it is difficult to model such emotional relationships with scientific modeling, whether we're talking God or human as the recipient of such affection. While emotional relationships are not easy to model using science, metaphorical models do seem fitting. I will not agree that emotion is ultimately beyond science—for many reasons, including the fact that emotion is just experimentally more difficult to reproduce in the laboratory; however, the emotional factor is not the main problem in modeling God. The problem is the observability of the target thing to be modeled. A target human being that is loved, honored, or glorified is quite observable, as is the behavior of the person doing the loving. A target God is not.

I can only conclude that currently there is no satisfactory way to model such a construct as God, since there is no credible way to specify God as distinguished from anything else. So, on the premise that to be able to model is to have *public* knowledge, based on instrumental reasoning, such knowledge about God appears to be impossible, at least for now. Where God per se is not modelable, that assessment is not true of human behavior in the practice of religion.

CAN RELIGIOUS PRACTICE BE MODELED?

Modeling religious practice is an example of the second type of belief model: in this case, how and why people acquire belief in God and carry out their worship behavior. The object of modeling here would be to characterize the behavior of people with respect to religious belief and participation. One can distinguish models of people, how they acquire belief and practice religion, as contrasted to modeling the nature of the God concept per se. The distinction is subtle, and some might assert that there can be no God that exists other than how people actively express what they believe and how they behave with respect to that belief.

With regard to the attributes and properties of the models cited earlier, religious practice is a very different story from the concept or nature of God per se. Religious practice surely can be modeled by science and has been. To be sure, there is already a significant literature on the topic, sometimes called sociology of religion; however, I would claim that scientific probes of why people believe what they say they believe, and how they practice that belief, have been timid and not as penetrating as is justified by the importance of the subject in our society.

One of those regarded as a "new atheist," philosopher Daniel Dennett, sees religious practice as a natural phenomenon that can be studied by science, much as any other aspect of human behavior.[2] It is probably true that some people take offense at such a notion, in the same way that they did with the Kinsey report, the scientific study of human sexuality. Religion, like sex, is regarded by some as personal and private. One of Dennett's research challenges is to use his theory of memes to trace how religious tendencies and ideas spread from person to person, and even seek to maximize their own spread. For example, computer-based social networks are amenable to making such measurements; they are already being used to evaluate the spread of consumer preference, political commentary, etc.

Religion is already being subjected to certain kinds of scientific investigation. Demographic poll-taking about beliefs is part of that. Journals like *Skeptical Inquirer* publish investigations of reported near-death experiences of "seeing God," the efficacy of prayer, "religious miracles," etc. The proposed modeling criteria can normally be satisfied, the same as is true of any other social science, given that there are some specific behavioral events to measure so as to provide objective data.

It is true that many of the dependent measures will be subjective data, which probably means that researchers will have to use categorical data and can aspire to ordering metrics at the most. The robustness of the models will be evaluated in terms of effectiveness in saying how religious practices help or hinder feelings, mental health, economics, government or corporate policy, or international relations. Social penetration of any model would have to wait for the science to be done. My point is not that such studies have not been done, but that studies and models have not been done nearly to the extent that is warranted, considering how religion plays such an important role in many peoples' lives.

Not everyone agrees with Dennett. Dr. Richard Sloan, professor of behavioral medicine at Columbia University and author of the book *Blind Faith: The Unholy Alliance of Religion and Medicine*, claims that the problem with studying religion scientifically is that you do violence to the phenomenon by reducing it to basic elements that can be quantified. Accordingly, he claims, that makes for bad science and bad religion. To me this seems like a weak rationalization to shy away from critical thinking. As has been affirmed throughout this book, religion cannot be reduced to mathematics, but it would seem that measurements at the low end (nominal categorization and ordering) *can* be applied. We can certainly measure human time, and energy and dollars, spent on religious activities—these are objective data with cardinal metrics. And we can be systematic in using subjective scales and other psychometrics of belief and preference that are at the current frontier of economic and psychological modeling and behavioral economics.

So, with regard to the six attributes, all can be applied, depending on the aspect of religious practice being studied. There are plenty of observables: what people say and what they do inside and outside religious services. Observables can include physiological measures of feeling and words that are associated in conjunction with brain scans. There is room for single, as well as multidimensional, studies, for instance, factor analysis and correlation. Many measures would be categorical or ordered preference, but time and money measures do provide ample opportunity for cardinal measurement. Robustness and social penetration (acceptance) will depend on models yet to be developed; that future is hard to judge since so few models are out there. There is sure to be controversy since modeling in this arena tampers with strong feelings. In any case, models can be as concise as any other models in social science and anthropology.

Religious practice entails many decisions about how to spend time and money with certainty and uncertainty, and the contingent value associations, so many decision models of psychology and economics would seem to apply. There are game situations that impinge on morality, as described in chapter 22, for competitive game situations.

Part III

Belief Today

7

VARIETY OF BELIEF PERSPECTIVES

Tell all the truth, but tell it slant
Success in circuit lies
Too bright for our infirm delight
The truth's superb surprise
As lightning to the children eased
With explanation kind
The truth must dazzle gradually
Or every man be blind —Emily Dickinson, *Complete Poems*, 1955

God is a verb.—R. Buckminster Fuller, *No More Second Hand God*, 1963

Religion is an illusion, and it derives its strength from its readiness to fit with our instinctual wishes.—Sigmund Freud, *Lecture 35*

Earlier we discussed scientific models: concise, hard-edged logical representations of belief, many adaptable to quantification. This chapter moves to some diverse considerations on what it means to believe, why we believe, the history of believing, and the linguistic factors we must consider in such discussions. These are considerations with a softer edge that tend to be qualitative, are more debatable, and are without consensus among scholars.

Admittedly there is no obvious coherence between the topics in this chapter, although for me they are topics that somehow seem relevant to the discussion of belief in God. Following a look at several different perspectives on what it means to believe, the chapter considers the current demographics of Western religious belief, jumps to the question of creationism, and then deals in some detail with the "new atheism." Then it considers salient cosmological questions, as well as the new technology of virtual reality, suggesting that religious belief is a kind of virtual reality, having common elements with experiments on human subjects who can be shown to experience (and believe in) phenomena that physically do not exist. There follow discussions of metaphor, myth, and spirituality. Then comes a favorite quotation from the *Wall Street Journal* on evolution, a series of questions about churchgoer behavior, and a proposal on redefining the term "God" to complete the chapter.

Consider Emily Dickinson's famous phrase, "Tell all the truth but tell it slant."[1] Initially the reader of a belief statement written by someone else cannot understand the full implications of what the writer intended or is thinking. The statement cannot be absorbed in one bite. Nor can the writer appreciate where the readers are coming from, what life experience those readers have had that will affect their initial interpretation. Furthermore, no matter how sophisticated the writer, or how elaborate the statement, the whole truth of what the writer intended will never be told. Finally, the writer will never know the whole truth of whatever the statement is about. Much as any writer would aspire to tell "all the truth" about his belief, that is clearly not possible: It ends up being "slant."

A belief statement is a kind of model of the writer's belief. There is a common expression that all models are wrong, mostly because they are incomplete. They are necessarily limited to a small slice of the target reality of what is being modeled. The "gradual dazzling" of the truth of anyone's beliefs requires feedback, clarification, further two-way communication, and mental soaking time for both writer and reader.

A Jesuit priest named Gian-Carlo Colombo, who was advocatus Dei (advocate for God) for the Voltaire Society, a student philosophy discussion society at Oxford University in the 1950s, distinguished several meanings of the word "belief."[2] He proposed the most straightforward meaning to be "belief that . . .," meaning belief that a particular proposition is true. These beliefs can be measured by such simple questions as the following: Do you believe God exists? Or do you believe God can perform what we call miracles? If there is an expectation that the person questioned is telling the truth the questioner must accept the answer.

A different meaning of belief Colombo proposed to be "belief in . . .," for example, the following: Do you believe in the Bible? Do you believe in capitalism? Do you believe in Obama? In this case there is no question about whether these entities exist. The implied questions have to do with whether the person questioned agrees with and/or would follow the recommendations of the document, theory, or person. Colombo asserts that this is a stronger form of belief than "belief that . . ." about some proposition. The best way to test the "belief in . . ." is to gather evidence of how the person behaves—whether the behavior is consistent with what he/she says.

Colombo had a third category of belief he called *faith*, which in his paper obviously has to do with faith in God, a belief allegedly so strong that it becomes the driving force of one's life. He asserts that faith in God needs no justification, for if it did there would not be faith. He refers to it as based on "interior experience," rather than external perception, and argues against Kierkegaard as to whether it is necessarily subjective. Colombo states that faith in God, as he characterizes it, is conviction with objective certainty. Here is where I would have to disagree. Especially since there is no observable, it must be subjective, namely, belief in an idea. That one behaves *as though* an idea has a basis in reality does not make the idea objective.

Philosophers, logicians, economists, and others too numerous to review have been proffering theories of belief for decades. From the ancient Greek philosophers until today there have been lively philosophical arguments about whether we believe based on rationality or emotion. For example, philosopher David Hume (1711–1776) claimed, "Reason is and ought only to be the slave of the passions."[3] Allegedly he was referring to one's innate sense of morality, that in dealing with moral issues one cannot reason independently of one's passions. We know that emotion plays a large role in belief, whether in a moral context or not.

Charles Sanders Peirce (1839–1914) characterized inquiry not so much as an effort to gain truth, but as a means to avoid doubts, social disagreement, and irritation, so as to reach a belief on the basis of which one is prepared to act.[4] He distinguished several approaches to inquiry: sticking to some original belief to bring comfort and decisiveness (he called this *tenacity*); being brutally authoritarian and trying to dominate others who offer contrary evidence (he called this *authority*); conformity with current paradigms, taste, and fashion, that is, what is more respectable (he called this *congruity*); and finally the method of science, which seeks to criticize, correct, and improve upon itself. I suppose real human inquiry is a blend of all of these modes.

G. E. Moore (1873–1958) posed the following paradox, namely, that people are inclined to say things like, "It is raining, but I can't believe it is raining," which is patently absurd but nevertheless logically consistent.[5] This led Moore to assert that one cannot believe falsely, although one can speak of someone else that they believe falsely.

Modern economic and cognitive science has worked hard to formalize models of belief. It continues to be recognized that belief is not simply a matter of being rational and having a straightforward way to draw conclusions about what is true and what is not. If one knows the probabilities associated with various kinds of observable evidence (the probability of a particular observation given that a particular hypothesis is true) there is a well-known mathematical model called Bayes's theorem that works well to estimate the truth or falsity of premises.[6] But the problem is that those contingent probabilities are subjective and only vaguely held in mind. This goes for both the mental formulation of the hypothesis and the estimation of probability contingent on each hypothesis. Some hypotheses may be well formed mentally along with some basis for estimating their probabilities, while some other plausible hypotheses may be overlooked or offer no hint of their probability. In using a Bayesian approach, a "don't know" category is often treated as indifference, with 50–50 probability belief. But some belief analysts rebel against interpreting "don't know" as a 50–50 probability estimation and regard that judgment as very different from making a probability assessment.

There has been recent formal (logical, mathematical) work on belief called Dempster–Shafer belief theory.[7] It is a generalization of Bayes's theorem cited earlier as one of the example models concerning statistical inference from evidence. It differs from Bayes's theorem in that the procedure is not limited to subjective probability judgments directly on the proposition. Rather, it is based on deriving degrees of belief for a given proposition from subjective judgments for both *strength of belief* and *judgment of plausibility* regarding various other questions (sets of *possibilities*) that contain the proposition. For example, a set of four possibilities might be: (1) X is true, (2) X is false, (3) X is neither true nor false, and (4) X is either true or false. There is a rule in Dempster–Shafer theory for combining multiple such degrees of belief when they are based on elements of evidence that are mutually independent. The degree of belief in the main proposition depends on the answers to related questions and the subjective probability of each answer.

There is the further, previously mentioned problem of what are called *unknown unknowns*, the "unk-unks." Some relevant properties are known as *credible variables*, that is, previously observed and identified as variables, their values unknown. Other properties have never been known or considered: the unk-unks. The believer or modeler simply has no thought of their existence or their relation to the issue at hand. This suggests that formal belief models should include two components: (1) the current state of belief, and (2) a rule for how current belief would be updated in light of new variables and new evidence. Unfortunately, the second component is missing in most cases.

Today, unquestionably, the norm is professed belief in God, with a variety of justifications. Some form of William James's (1842–1910) "inner personal experience" is most often cited, or the Bible or the Quran, as tradition or revelation, with tacit agreement that material observable evidence of God is rather sparse. Many clergy emphasize with R. Buckminster Fuller that, "God is a verb," that belief is verified only by active seeking, faith, and acceptance; however, many others, probably a gradually increasing number, will agree with Freud, that the "instinctual wish" for help from above, for a loving and all-powerful father figure, is the primary driving force. A religious person might claim that this is how God makes Himself manifest.

Michael Shermer (1954–), founder of the Skeptics Society and editor of its magazine, *Skeptic*, recites the following conversation as typical of many he has experienced:

"What triggered the Big Bang?"
    "God did it."
    "Who created God?"
    "God is He who needs not be created."
    "Why can't the universe be that which needs not be created?"
    "The universe is a thing or event, whereas God is an agent or being, and things and events have to be created by something, but an agent or being does not."
    "Isn't God a thing or being if he is part of the universe?"
    "God is not a thing, God is an agent or being."
    "Don't agents or beings have to be created as well? We're an agent or being—a human being in fact. We agree that human beings need an

explanation for our origin. So why does this causal reasoning not apply to God as an agent or being?"

"God is outside of time, space, and matter, and thus needs no explanation."

"In that case it is not possible for any of us to know if there is a God or not because, by definition, as finite beings operating exclusively within the world, we can only know other natural and finite beings and objects. It is not possible for a finite natural being to know a supernatural infinite being."[8]

At this point in the conversation my erstwhile theological opponents typically turn to ancillary argument, for instance, personal revelation, which by definition is personal and thus cannot serve as evidence to others who have not shared that revelatory experience.

Shermer goes on to point out, as have many others throughout time, that the burden of proof is on believers to prove the existence of God, not on nonbelievers to disprove it. To date, he claims that theists have failed to prove God's existence, at least by the high evidentiary standards of science and reason.

8

DEMOGRAPHICS AND TRENDS

We all know that in surveys about anything, the way the question is posed has a great effect on the answer. Professional pollsters take great pains to sample as randomly as they can and offer percentages from a large enough sample that there is credible statistical significance. With those caveats, here are some data from various sources taken in recent years.

First some recent data from Gallup. In 2001, 2004, 2007, and 2016, Gallup asked a separate question that gave Americans three options to characterize their beliefs: "believe in," "not sure about," and "don't believe in." In 2001 and 2004, 90 percent of U.S. adults said they believed in God, with 7 percent and 5 percent, respectively, saying they were unsure. By 2007, the percentage choosing "believe in God" had dropped slightly to 86 percent, with another 8 percent expressing uncertainty. In 2016, "believe in God" dropped further to 79 percent, with 10 percent unsure. Still, the 89 percent who said they believed in God or were unsure (as opposed to saying they don't believe in God) was the same as the 89 percent who responded affirmatively when asked the simpler "yes or no" question, "Do you believe in God?" Gallup also asked the question that included the "not sure about" option in random rotation with questions about belief in four other religious concepts: angels, heaven, hell, and the devil. Americans' belief in all of these was lower than their belief in God, ranging from 72 percent who said they believe in angels to 61 percent who said they believe in the devil, with 12 percent unsure on both. Belief in these four concepts was down at least marginally from when last measured in 2007, following the same pattern as the trend in belief in God using this question format.[1]

A 2012 Gallup poll indicated that 46 percent believed that God created man in his current form, while 32 percent of the respondents held the belief that humans evolved through the guidance of God.[2] A 2019 Gallup poll found that since 1999, the number of adults in the United States with no "religious affiliation" went from 8 to 19 percent.[3] Actual membership in a particular church is a different story, with roughly 50 percent of adults claiming they do not belong. Among Catholics, church membership during this period went from 76 to 63 percent, and for protestants from 73 to 67 percent. For Hispanics, membership dropped from 68 to 45 percent. With regard to political affiliation, for Democrats church membership dropped from 71 to 48 percent, and for Republicans from 77 to 69 percent. The margin of error is claimed to be roughly 3 percent. According to analysts the correlation between religiosity and being Republican has actually increased throughout the years. Figure 8.1 tables some of the data.[4]

Considering some older (and quainter) data, in a March 24, 1997, Yankelovich survey of 1,018 participants reported in *Time Magazine*, 81 percent of those surveyed believed in heaven and 67 percent in hell. Thirty-four percent believed that they go to heaven because of faith in God, 6 percent because of good things that they do, and 57 percent both. Sixty-seven percent believed heaven is "up there." Sixty-one percent believed they will go to heaven, while 1 percent believed they will go to hell. Five percent believed in reincarnation and 4 percent in the end of all existence. Ninety-three percent believed angels are in heaven, 79 percent

	BELIEVE IN	NOT SURE ABOUT	DON'T BELIEVE IN
	%	%	%
God	79	10	11
Angels	72	12	16
Heaven	71	14	15
Hell	64	13	22
The Devil	61	12	27

Figure 8.1.   Polling data from Gallup. *Author's drawing*

believed that there they will encounter St. Peter, 43 percent believed they will find harps in heaven, and 36 percent believed there will be halos. Eighty-eight percent believed they will meet friends and family members in heaven. A more recent AP-GFK poll in 2011, claimed that the belief in angels was down to 77 percent.[5]

According to ARIS (American Religious Identification Survey), in 2001, the largest gain in church membership since 1990 was "evangelical born-again" (42 percent), while self-proclaimed nondenominationals totaled 37 percent. The others had no religion (23 percent).[6] According to a 2008 national poll by the Pew Research Center for the People and the Press, a sharply rising percentage of people age 30 and younger, from the so-called Millennial Generation, are coming to doubt the existence of God and Judgment Day.[7]

A 2012 Pew survey found that belief in the existence of God has dropped 15 points in the last five years among Americans age 30 and younger. Pew, which has been studying that trend for 25 years, found that just 68 percent of millennials in 2012 agreed with the statement, "I never doubt the existence of God," down from 76 percent in 2009 and 83 percent in 2007. Among other generations, belief in God is high and has seen few changes in recent decades. Between 81 and 89 percent of older generations say they never doubt the existence of God. The older the generation, the more likely they are to believe in God.[8]

A 2011 study by the Pew Forum on Religion and Public Life provided interesting data differentiating religious groups in the United States with respect to both college education and annual income (see figure 8.2).[9] This is not meant to suggest that we should all become Hindus or reformed Jews; one might suspect that the data are conditioned on where the sample was taken and the circumstances that led to certain ethnic groups doing well.

According to a recent (2012) European study, 47 percent of Frenchmen declared themselves to be agnostic. European countries in general have experienced a decline in church membership and church attendance. A relevant example is Sweden, where the Church of Sweden, previously the state-church until 2000, claimed to have 82.9 percent of the Swedish population as its flock in 2000. But surveys there showed this had dropped to 72.9 percent by 2008; however, in the 2005 Eurobarometer poll, only 23 percent of the Swedish population said they believed in a personal God. The Eurobarometer poll found that, on average, 52 percent

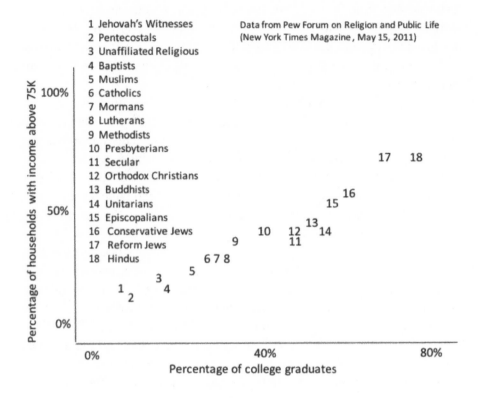

**Figure 8.2.   Comparison of U.S. religious groups with respect to college gradua-
tion and annual income.** *Author's drawing*

of the citizens of European Union member states stated that they "believe
in God" and 27 percent believed there is some sort of spirit or life force,
while 18 percent did not believe there is any sort of spirit, God, or life
force. Among other categories 3 percent declined to answer. [10]

A 2012 survey by Ipsos Social Research Institute, a global research
company, showed that only 51 percent of people throughout the world
believed in God. Eighteen percent didn't believe, and 17 percent were
undecided. More than 18,000 people in 23 countries participated in that
London-based poll. The Ipsos poll also found that 51 percent believed
there is an afterlife, while 23 percent believed they will just "cease to
exist." About a quarter (26 percent) said they simply don't know what
will happen after death. [11]

Clearly, the United States has more believers, at least those who tell
pollsters they are believers, than the rest of the world. I suspect that the

trend of disbelief will continue worldwide. The numbers clearly show a diversity of belief, with a strong dependence on how the question is posed and who is being asked.

9

IS CREATIONISM DEAD?

Many school districts, particularly in the U.S. Bible Belt states, have voted to teach creationism alongside evolution, based on the premise that both are "just theories." The retort, which most of us agree with, is that the evidence for the theory of Darwinian evolution is overwhelming and becoming ever more so, whereas the evidence for creationism is nil by scientific standards. Theories have no meaning without evidence to support them, presumably codified in terms of understandable models.

In 1999, the U.S. National Academy of Sciences published a report titled *Science and Creationism*, criticizing creationism as posing an alternative to evolution. The report states, that scientists, like many others, are touched with awe at the order and complexity of nature. Indeed, many scientists are deeply religious.[1] They note that many believe that science and religion are two separate realms of human experience, and that, "Demanding that they be combined detracts from the glory of each." I would certainly agree that they are commonly regarded as two separate realms of human *experience*. But whether they should be two separate realms of human *thought* is a different question.

In 2008, the National Academy of Sciences was further alarmed by the propensity of some states and communities to pass laws that creationism should be taught to schoolchildren alongside evolution. They gathered a broad spectrum of scientists and educators, and published a second report, *Science, Evolution, and Creationism*.[2] The main conclusion of this report is that evolution is an accepted fact based on overwhelming evidence broadly accepted by the science community very different from religion, which is based on faith. They conclude that creationism has no place in science education.

10

THE NEW ATHEISM

During the last few years, there has been a surge of books and magazine articles advocating atheism. Among the most celebrated authors are the already mentioned Oxford University evolutionist Richard Dawkins, Tufts University philosopher Daniel Dennett, University of California neuroscientist Sam Harris, and physicist Victor Stenger. In addition are prolific journalist Christopher Hitchins,[1] State University of New York at Buffalo philosopher Paul Kurtz,[2] and many others. There have long been other proponents of atheism within the academic or philosophy communities, for instance, philosopher Michael Martin. What characterizes these newer authors is their outspoken urge to bring religion into the spotlight of rational observation and critique, and the feeling that for too long religion has been accepted and tolerated as a social practice that has been assumed to be off limits from investigation. What is especially interesting is that the challenges are coming from diverse academic disciplines, including biology and physics, as well as philosophy.

Most of what the "new atheists" are saying is not new. Many of the arguments were made by those previously mentioned in the book. Perhaps the new atheists are simply adding a contemporary slant and helping atheism gain momentum.

GRAY'S SEVEN TYPES OF ATHEISM

John Gray, professor of politics at Oxford University, authored a new book called *Seven Types of Atheism*.[3] He claims to have been inspired to write his book by a categorization described in a reputable book by poetry critic William Empson called *Seven Types of Ambiguity*.[4] Gray's seven types can be seen to be parallel or analogous to Empson's, so they are detailed here for the curious reader to compare. (I find them a stretch.)

Empson's categories are as follows:

1. Metaphor, when two things are said to be alike that have different properties.
2. When two or more meanings are resolved into one, for example, using two different metaphors at once.
3. When two ideas that are connected through context can be given in one word simultaneously.
4. When two or more meanings that do not agree are combined to try to make clear a complicated state of mind in the author.
5. When the author discovers his idea in the act of writing, for example, a simile that lies halfway between two statements made by the author.
6. When a statement says nothing and the readers are forced to invent a statement of their own, most likely in conflict with that of the author.
7. When two words that within context are opposites that expose a fundamental division in the author's mind.

Gray emulated Empson's taxonomy with the following characterization of atheism:

1. That "new atheism" contains little that is interesting or different from old atheism.
2. That "humanism" is a hollowed-out version of the Christian belief in the salvation of history.
3. A kind of atheism that makes religion from science, including evolutionary humanism and dialectical materialism.
4. Modern "political religions": including Nazism and contemporary evangelical liberalism.
5. God haters like the Marquis de Sade.

6. Atheisms of Joseph Conrad and George Santayana.
7. The "mystical atheisms" of Arthur Schopenhauer and the negative theologies of Benedict Spinoza.

Gray expresses his own preference for the last two categories, which are happy to live in a "godless world or an un-nameable God."[5] A principal argument by Gray is that the God of monotheism did not die, but only left the scene for a while, to reappear as "humanity." Gray claims that a philosophy called "humanity" is a work of the imagination and that the only observable reality is the multitudinous human animal, with its conflicting goals, values, and ways of life. Whereas old-fashioned monotheism had the merits of admitting that very little can be known of God, we can question how much can be known or, in particular, how much faith we can have in the "phantom of humanity." Gray asserts that the grandiose theories of today's atheists have been inherited from positivism as science advances. He claims that atheists who demonize religion will face a problem of evil as insoluble as that which faces Christianity. Gray claims that if you want to understand atheism and religion you must forget the popular notion that they are opposites. Thus, he sees contemporary atheism as a continuation of monotheism by other means. Belief and unbelief are poses the mind adopts in the face of unimaginable reality.

DOES EVOLUTION POINT TO GOD?

The theory of evolution, ever since Charles Darwin (1809–1882), has raised serious questions about the existence of God. Darwin held off on publishing *The Origin of Species* for years after returning from his voyage on the HMS *Beagle* (mid-1830s). He published in 1859, still conflicted in his own mind about the implications of what he had discovered. Darwin had studied at Cambridge to become an Anglican minister, although his family was made up of Unitarian freethinkers. The theory of natural selection emerged in 1838, from his studies of the evidence he had gathered.[6] Darwin was writing his theory in 1858, when Alfred Russel Wallace sent him an essay in which he posited a similar theory.[7] Some claim that Wallace should get more credit for the theory of evolution than he has received. The implications for theology of Darwin's book were fairly obvious almost immediately.

Many scholars of evolution have since suggested that evolution does not point to any God. Richard Dawkins (1941–) of Oxford has been the most vocal of these and has published and spoken widely in recent years. In his book *The Blind Watchmaker*, he takes issue with the 1802 argument propounded by theist William Paley (1743–1805) that design (e.g., of a wristwatch) implies the existence of an intelligent designer, and therefore the design of living forms implies the existence of a God.[8] Dawkins details how through natural selection evolution allows complex living organisms to come into being, requiring nothing but chance (and time for evolution to play out). In *The God Delusion*, he argues that religious faith is a delusion.[9] The latter book, published in 2006, sold several million copies by 2010.

As might be expected, Dawkins's book elicited a strong protest from theist philosophers like Notre Dame's Alvin Plantinga (1932–). He has stated, "You really can't sensibly claim theistic belief is irrational without showing it isn't true." And that, he argues, is simply beyond what science can do. Plantinga says he accepts the scientific theory of evolution, as all Christians should. The new atheists, he argues, are the ones who are misreading Darwin. Their belief that evolution rules out the existence of God—including a God who purposely created human beings through a process of guided evolution—is not a scientific claim, he writes, but a "metaphysical or theological addition."[10]

Francis Collins (1950–), former head of the U.S. government's Human Genome Project, is a deeply religious man. He expresses the view in *The Language of God* that faith in science and faith in God are not inconsistent.[11] Being a genetic biologist, he cannot run away from evolution, but he repudiates the atheistic view held by many scholars of evolution. He starts from the assumption of God and assumes that evolution was created by God. In the process, he admits that belief in God requires a leap in faith in a God that is outside of nature.

The point made by the atheistic evolutionists to counter theists like Plantinga and Collins is that the hypothesis of God is simply not necessary to explain the facts of evolution. Darwin explained the mechanism, and there is no need to invoke God. The God construct has no explanatory value. Mathematician Pierre Simon Laplace (1749–1827) said it many years earlier in response to a query from Napoleon: "I have no need for that hypothesis."

IS GOD NEEDED AS A BASIS FOR MORALITY?

Philosophers have long argued about whether there is a basis for morality other than religion. Michael Martin (1932–2015), in *Theism, Morality, and Meaning*, offers numerous arguments, stated as syllogisms, to assert that secular reasons can easily provide motivation for atheists to be moral.[12] The most plausible theory to explain the meaning of ethical expressions, he claims, is what is called *ideal observer theory* (originally put forth by Roderick Firth in 1970), where a human observer who is fully informed and impartial makes judgments of approval or disapproval. This, however, seems to beg the question, who among us can ever be fully informed and impartial?

Sam Harris (1967–), a philosopher and neuroscientist, has authored several books supporting atheism, including *The End of Faith, Letter to a Christian Nation*, and *The Moral Landscape*.[13] With regard to the last book, most people, whether believers or not, feel that science has little to say about moral values and that this failure explains in large part why people turn to religion. Harris confronts this issue directly, claiming that human (and animal and plant) well-being is the only legitimate basis for moral values and that science has a lot to say about this relationship. It will take time to overcome the cultural inertia, but Harris believes that in due time science will be able to tell us right from wrong, and how we *ought* to behave, in addition to how we do behave. He points out, as every scientist already understands, that there is no such thing as Christian or Muslim mathematics. He asserts that science can eventually bring us together regarding a basis for morality.

GOD OF THE GAPS

In its 2008 report on creationism, the National Academy of Sciences steers clear of answering whether science disproves religion, noting that many theologians oppose a "God of the gaps" approach (that everything not explainable by science can be left for a supernatural God) because that notion undermines faith.[14] Actually, the God of the gaps idea has been around since 1904, when Scottish evangelist, writer, and lecturer Henry Drummond (1851–1897) developed the concept in his *Lowell Lectures on the Ascent of Man*.[15] He chastised Christians who emphasize things that science cannot yet explain—"gaps which they will fill up with God." He urged them to embrace all nature as the work of the "God of Evolution, [who] is infinitely grander than the occasional wonder-worker."[16]

"God of the gaps" has become a popular term for bashing skeptics of God; however, later I will attempt to resurrect the term as a reasonable way to redefine what we mean by God. It simply changes the definition of God: not a supernatural person, but rather the total set of phenomena that we simply do not understand.

BREAKING THE SPELL

Another major figure in the so-called new atheist movement is philosopher Daniel Dennett (1942–) of Tufts University. In his book *Breaking the Spell*, Dennett refers to the "spell" that religion has on people everywhere and the prevalent inhibition from undertaking scientific investigation of the practice of religion—that religion is somehow off limits.[17] He discusses *memes*, ideas that are handed down and evolve in the community in a manner analogous to genes, as described in Dawkins's *The Selfish Gene*.[18] The implication is that religious ideas are memes handed down from ancient folklore. Dennett has popularized the interesting term "belief in belief." In other words, people feel they are expected (by friends, family, community, other social associations) to believe (or act as though they believe), and so "believing" would be to their social advantage.

Certainly, religious affiliation and belief have been polled, doctrines of various religious institutions have been studied and compared, and thousands of books critical of religion have been written. But Dennett focuses on scientific inquiry of religion, involving well-designed experiments, experimental controls, etc.

Leon Wieseltier (1952–) accuses Dennett of believing "in the grossest biologism or in the grossest theism, in a purely naturalistic understanding of religion or in intelligent design, in the omniscience of a white man with a long beard in nineteenth-century England" and that "not all aspects of human life can or should be illuminated by science."[19] Harvard biologist/evolutionist Edward O. Wilson (1929–) believes that notions of God and rituals of religion are a result of human evolution. He agrees with

Dennett that religion should be studied using scientific methodology. He argues that religious practices do confer biological advantage through the reduction of reality to images and definitions that are easily understood and difficult to refute. He sees commitment through faith as a kind of tribalism enacted through self-surrender. He claims that myth is used to assert the tribe's favored position on the Earth, with supernatural forces providing control and promising apocalypse. He doubts that religion can be easily replaced by scientific materialism and argues that, because science and religion are two of the most potent forces on Earth, theists and scientists should work toward an alliance. [20]

Neuroscientists, including Sam Harris, have suggested that study of the brain will eventually have much to say about religion. Geneticist Dean Hamer (1951–) authored the book *The God Gene: How Faith Is Hardwired into Our Genes*. [21] He refers to a gene called VMAT2, which has been associated with mystical experiences. Hamer proposes that spirituality and "self-transcendence" can be measured by psychometric experiments, and that the tendency to be spiritual can be inherited.

Critics of Hamer have complained that his conclusions are premature and irresponsible, and that no single gene can account for religion, that it is tied to culture and many other factors. Such theists as Anglican priest John Polkinghorne (1930–)[22] complain that Hamer's contentions reveal the poverty in reductionist thinking. [23] But many people believe that neurological research will eventually shed light on religious experience.

ONE PHYSICIST'S PERSPECTIVE

Victor Stenger (1935–), an American particle physicist, has played an active role in the new atheist movement, with several books, the most popular of which is *God, the Failed Hypothesis*. [24] The premise is that if God created the universe, there must be some evidence for that, and none has been found; however, if a properly controlled experiment revealed hard scientific evidence for God, that would change science in fundamental ways. He discusses reports of mystical experiences, experiments on intercessory prayer and near-death experiences, etc., but there is no evidence that passes muster in terms of what is credible according to the consensual criteria of science outlined earlier.

In the preface of his book *The New Atheism*, Stenger comments, "The very ideal of religious tolerance—born of the notion that every human being should be free to believe whatever he wants about God—is one of the principle forces driving us toward the abyss" (acceptance that belief should be arbitrary).[25] His point is that truth is not arbitrary and people are obliged to consider the prevailing evidence and the rationality of competing models of what is true—and discard those that are evidently false. (That is a grand hope but one not easily achieved. Furthermore, different beliefs can be legitimately based on different peoples' experiences. That is not arbitrary.)

11

THE BIG BANG, THE MULTIVERSE, AND A NEW DISCONTINUITY IN OUR PERCEIVED IMPORTANCE

It seems appropriate to present in this chapter a brief update on what many physicists are now agreeing to in regard to the origins of everything. Ancient peoples were afraid to venture outside their own universe, the tribal village, not knowing what existed there or what harm would befall them if they searched. Many years later it seemed obvious to most everyone that the Earth was flat, and if explorers sailed too far they might fall off the edge. There were a few (like Aristarchus and Euclid in about 300 BC) who spoke of a round Earth. Eventually, explorers figured out that the world was indeed round, but it appeared that the round world was all that existed, save some twinkling things in the heavens where the gods dwelt. Then astronomers pieced together notions that there are other planets like our own out there, in orbits around our common sun. Later it was revealed that those twinkling things, the stars, were really suns, around which there were other planets, all in a common galaxy that we now call the Milky Way. Then our telescopes became powerful enough to see other galaxies. Typical galaxies range from dwarfs with as few as 10 million (10^7) stars to giants with 100 trillion (10^{14}) stars, all orbiting the galaxy's center of mass. At each stage of discovery, the perception of the role of humanity was diminished both physically and psychologically relative to the rest of the known universe.

Let's examine some specifics of our universe. The Big Bang is a good place to start (allegedly that actually *was* the start).

THE BIG BANG, AND OTHER THEORIES OF THE UNIVERSE'S ORIGIN

Physicists estimate that the so-called big bang, the sudden expansion and cooling of matter that physicists regard as the beginning of our universe, occurred 13.7 billion years ago. This number is based in part on thermal measurements of cosmic radiation and cooling by the 2001 NASA spacecraft called the Wilkinson Microwave Anisotropy Probe. It is also based on Edwin Hubble's 1920 observation that the farther out in the universe we look, the redder the light. That means, according to the Doppler effect, that the longer the wavelength (i.e., the redder), the faster the velocity of the galactic light sources moving away from us, which in turn enables a backward calculation to the big bang.[1]

Contemporary theories further indicate that space as we know it is itself expanding, that is, the universe is not expanding "into" anything outside of itself. The three Nobel Prize laureates who were announced in 2012, solidified the evidence and attributed the cause to the repulsive force of "dark energy" (whatever that is) that is continually accelerating the expansion.

The expansion of space is presumably pushing back on the photons emanating from outer space as they travel toward us, thus impeding their apparent velocity. As one account on the web puts it, "In effect, the light reaching us has to fight its way upstream against expanding space."[2] An analogy would be an ant crawling along a rubber band toward us (at the speed of light relative to the rubber band) at the same time as the rubber band (space) is being stretched. While Einstein's special relativity constrains objects in the universe from moving faster than the speed of light with respect to one another, there is no such theoretical constraint when space itself is expanding; therefore, those most distant galaxies we can see with the Hubble telescope, at the edge of our observable universe, are much more distant than the 13.7 light-years away that would be the case were space stable. The current estimate is that the "edge" of the observable universe is roughly 42 billion light-years away.[3] The universe could be bigger. Light from the most distant stars may still not have had time to reach us since the big bang.

What happened "before" the big bang is a subject of much speculation. One theory, attributable to cosmologists Alan Guth and Sean Carroll, is that the universe collapsed into a point before it expanded in the big bang. Another, associated with Alex Valenkin, James Hartle, and Stephen Hawking, is that the universe appeared out of nothing and that no external forces were necessary.[4] Allegedly the strange properties of quantum physics allowed this something-from-nothing to happen. By the way, time, at the origin point, is nonexistent according to Einstein. There was no "before."[5] So much for the role of God "before" the big bang.

THE MULTIVERSE

As if the expansion of space were not strange enough, in the last decade cosmologists have been proposing a seemingly much more bizarre idea, published in reputable journals and books, and extrapolated from already established theories of physics, that there are multiple universes out there. That is to say, where our own universe is normally defined by all that exists that obeys laws of physics as we know them, there are other universes that exist and follow very different physical laws. *Scientific American* has undertaken a series of articles on the subject.[6] Allegedly, these theories are largely based on what is regarded as the most comprehensive theory of nature, string theory, which allows as many as 11 dimensions (well beyond our intuitive notions of three dimensions of space and one of time). There is nothing intuitive about string theory.

The multiverses the physicists describe are not empirically observable and would seem never to be. They are theoretical extrapolations of the known physics. The only operable criterion of these theories is internal mathematical consistency extrapolated from where we do have real data. Different individual theorists are coming up with different multiverse theories. Any one theory can be discredited if some logical inconsistency is found starting from known data.

Some believe that there is great diversity of universes, the laws of physics being quite different from one such universe to another. That would help explain the remarkable fact mentioned earlier that the physical constants of our particular universe have just the right values for complex molecules to sustain life—a chance occurrence within the large random distribution of multiple universes. (Reminder: The improbable set of constants that permit life is a principal reason some modern theologians give for the existence of God.) But the problem is that the idea of "God" has no explanatory value, while a mathematically plausible notion is that by chance, we are lucky to live in a universe with friendly physical constants, one among a large random set of universes having different properties. It would almost appear that string theory, which many physicists accept, seems to allow almost anything to be true. Cosmology scientists are working hard to find a grand unifying explanation to replace the current hodgepodge of separate arguments for the same cosmic phenomena.

A FIFTH DISCONTINUITY?

In a 1995 book entitled *The Fourth Discontinuity*, Massachusetts Institute of Technology (MIT) historian Bruce Mazlish (1923–) portrays four breaks, or "discontinuities," in man's perceived importance in our physical environment.[7] The first discontinuity was spatial, that being Copernicus' revelation that we humans are not at the geometric center of things. Mazlish's second discontinuity came with Darwin's discovery of evolution: that we are descended from lower creatures. The third discontinuity was Freud's construct of the superego and the id posing on both sides of the conscious ego: that we are not consciously in control of our own behavior. Mazlish's fourth discontinuity is the thesis that machines are gradually overtaking people in ability to sense, respond with speed and power, and "think."

With regard to the latter, there is no question about the machine's ability to sense well beyond human capability and move with greater speed and power. While there are plenty of arguments about what "thinking" means, the superiority of the computer has been amply demonstrated, certainly by IBM's Big Blue computer beating the world's best human chess champion, and then by their computer named Watson beating the world's best players of the game show *Jeopardy*.

With new theories from cosmologists about multiple universes, maybe infinite in number, we humans are confronted with a further decline in our status. That trend suggests that humankind is experiencing (at least) a fifth discontinuity and concomitant decline in how important we are in the grander scheme of things. Maybe this is comeuppance for our hubris in thinking that we humans are special and have any basis for knowing anything about God.

IS SCIENCE JUST ANOTHER RELIGION?

This question is often asked and answered in the affirmative by theists. Since what one accepts as a starting premise determines to a large extent what one concludes is true downstream, I suppose science *is* a kind of religion. And it is a religion that since the eighteenth-century enlightenment has gradually been winning out; however, its starting premises are very different from those of any other religion.

Totally unlike any other religion, the methods of science include a built-in effort to disprove that any particular current hypothesis is true, and that effort is exercised seriously and continuously. Those hypotheses and premises that withstand this test are regarded as *provisional* truth, always *conditional* upon new evidence that forces modification. Scientists throughout the world, from different cultural backgrounds, readily participate in and respect this process. For those who participate, the religion of science knows no cultural boundaries.

Effort by other "religions" is just the opposite: to reinforce belief in whatever is the professed doctrine. Thus, religious doctrine perpetuates itself from generation to generation, resisting new evidence and criticism. In stark contrast, the approach of science is open to new evidence, self-criticism, and refinement. The approach of religion is based on defense of faith. Within science the faith is in the method of being skeptical. In this critical sense, science and religion are not compatible.

DO THE MAGISTERIA OVERLAP?

Evolutionary biologist Stephen Jay Gould (1941–2002), in his book *Rock of Ages*, speaks of science and religion as "nonoverlapping *magisteria*," where he defines *magisterium* as a "domain where one form of teaching holds the appropriate tools for meaningful discourse and resolution." The idea is that science uses empiricism to specify facts about the physical universe and scientific theory to say why it is made as it is, whereas religion deals with questions of ultimate meaning and moral value.

In an earlier (1997) speech to the American Institute of Biological Science, Gould stated,

Religion is too important to too many people for any dismissal or denigration of the comfort still sought by many folks from theology. I may, for example, privately suspect that papal insistence on divine infusion of the soul represents a sop to our fears, a device for maintaining a belief in human superiority within an evolutionary world offering no privileged position to any creature. But I also know that souls represent a subject outside the magisterium of science. My world cannot prove or disprove such a notion, and the concept of souls cannot threaten or impact my domain. Moreover, while I cannot personally accept the Catholic view of souls, I surely honor the metaphorical value of such a concept both for grounding moral discussion and for expressing what we most value about human potentiality: our decency, care, and all the ethical and intellectual struggles that the evolution of consciousness imposed upon us.

This view has faced heavy criticism from Dawkins, who contends, as does Harris, that the divide between science and religion is not so simple. He disagrees with the premise that science has little meaningful to say about ethics and values. Dawkins has stated,

It is completely unrealistic to claim, as Gould and many others do, that religion keeps itself away from science's turf, restricting itself to morals and values. A universe with a supernatural presence would be a fundamentally and qualitatively different kind of universe from one without. The difference is, inescapably, a scientific difference. Religions make existence claims, and this means scientific claims.[8]

Clearly the divide was more credible in an earlier culture and way of thinking, when science and rationality held lesser sway in philosophy. Dawkins makes the additional interesting point that not all grammatically correct questions deserve an answer, giving as an example a question: "What does the color red smell like?" He goes on to assert that if DNA evidence suggested that Jesus had an earthly father, then Gould's claim of nonoverlapping magisteria would have to be dropped.

This writer's opinion is that Gould was influenced by wanting to be diplomatic, recognizing, as I do, that many people have deeply held religious beliefs, and offending them may not be a productive way to persuade. They are comfortable respecting science and striving for rationality in their weekday pursuits, while respecting religion on weekends as a different category of belief. But some of us find it difficult to entertain two different belief systems that are in conflict.

12

APPREHENDING REALITY

VIRTUAL REALITY

We now come to a current topic that impinges on the salient question of what we perceive to be reality. The reader may be well aware of the term "virtual reality" (VR), meaning the art of producing the experience of seeing, hearing, and feeling what is not really there. We refer to the new technology of computerized animation in TV ads, movies, and computer games. How does that topic relate to modeling our beliefs about real objects and events? The answer is that there is a rich vein of research and understanding of how people perceive reality, emanating from experiments with so-called virtual reality technology. This writer has been involved in VR research, and it is for that reason that I see a connection to the question of apprehending reality, and even modeling God.

First let us admit that the term "virtual reality" is an oxymoron, a self-contradiction from the normal use of English words. If something is virtual it is not real, and if it is real it is not virtual. But the term has caught on and is in the current vernacular, so we will use it; however, it might be noted that "virtual environment" is perhaps a more precise phrase for what is meant.

Let us also reflect on the fact that in some primitive forms the art of eliciting a VR experience has been around for a long time. Verbal storytelling probably dates back to primitive peoples who lived in caves. One can easily imagine that good storytelling, whether to groups huddled around a campfire or children at bedtime, has always stirred the listeners and conjured up active and *realistic* mental images. After the invention of writing, there were depictions of battles and other events that actively provoked the reader's imagination. Later came the theater. Much more recently came radio, and who of us oldsters can forget such radio serials as *The Lone Ranger*, *The Shadow*, and other serial radio programs that kept listeners glued to the set, filling in for visual images that were not there. All of these communication media can be said to have elicited a VR experience.

To appreciate VR let's consider the dramatic technological advances that have come about in only a few years. VR technology has resulted from the fact that computers can be programmed to generate dynamic displays that are highly realistic, of people, animals, plants, vehicles, buildings—anything at all, in full color and with accurate motion. We are so accustomed to seeing such virtual computer-graphic images in TV advertisements that we are numb to the wonder of it all. But what makes for a far more compelling experience is new technology that lets the viewer *immerse* himself in a virtual environment. This is achieved by the participant wearing a head-mounted display, a helmet or eyeglasses that present to the viewer a computer-generated image. Since the helmet or eyeglasses have sensors that detect which way the head is pointing (up or down, left or right) the computer can sense this and make the computer-generated image be what the viewer *would* see if the head were oriented in the same way while viewing the real environment. This is very compelling and produces the striking sensation that VR researchers call "immersion" in the virtual environment.[1]

Auditory VR technology is such an old story that we do not recognize it as VR. Apart from storytelling on the radio we have electronically recorded music, enhanced to produce a stereo effect by using earphones or strategically placed loudspeakers corresponding to placement of microphones at the recording site. More recently a scientific understanding of how the shape of the ear enables us to distinguish sound behind or above the head has resulted in added electronics to replicate this effect. For example, a listener can be made to experience a virtual buzzing insect swirling around the head at easily identifiable locations, where the apparent insect location is produced electronically.

New technology also permits haptic immersion in a virtual environment, where the participant can experience the sense of touching objects in the environment that are not really there. How can this possibly be? It is achieved by having the participant wear a specially made glove that stimulates the tactile nerve endings on the skin in correspondence to whether the computer software indicates contact with an object at any particular location.

In addition to entertainment from TV and computer games there are many practical applications of virtual vision, hearing, touch, and force feedback. An earlier application was the flight simulator, used in pilot training. By suspending the pilot and the entire cockpit on a six-legged computer-moveable base, flight trainers are able to produce realistic roll, pitch, and yaw motion simulation (e.g., of midair turbulence). The resulting VR sensation can be made so true to that of flying the actual aircraft that in many cases no training in the actual aircraft is required before the pilot flies the actual aircraft with a load of passengers. Similar devices are now used for highway vehicle driver training. Another application is in the domain or design of machines or buildings, where the designer can view a computer-graphic representation of his design from any viewpoint at any angle, or the architect or his prospective customer can "walk through" a virtual building, look in any direction, and see what the designer put there—before any actual machine or building exists.

Using similar technology, the participant's hand can be placed within a mechanism that causes a remote hand/arm arbitrarily far away to touch or handle real objects. The human operator's hand can receive force feedback corresponding precisely to the forces the remote mechanical hand encounters in its environment. This technology for remote handling was originally applied to enable a human operator to peer through a leaded glass (shielded) window to manipulate objects in a nearby radioactively hot environment.[2] Without the virtual touch and force feedback it would be impossible to perform such remote manipulation safely and reliably.

Figure 12.1 illustrates the operation. The dashed line around the remote manipulator arm suggests that the remote arm can be either real or virtual, and that if the visual and/or tactile feedback is good enough there will be no difference in the human operator's perception (mental model, shown in the cloud) of the (real or virtual) reality.

Developments in remote manipulation have led to robotic surgery, where the surgeon views a TV image and performs the surgical manipulations by placing his hands in force and touch feedback devices. By the latter, he positions the miniature TV camera and steers the surgical tools

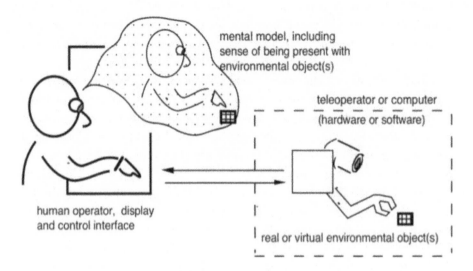

mental model, including
sense of being present with
environmental object(s)

teleoperator or computer
(hardware or software)

human operator, display
and control interface

real or virtual environmental object(s)

Figure 12.1.   Controlling a remote hand to grasp objects appears the same whether the environment is real or virtual. *Author's drawing*

inside the patient's body. For some delicate operations, movements can be "scaled down" so that movements in comfortable range for the human (e.g., inches) correspond to movements of a small fraction of an inch inside the patient. Manipulation control can similarly be "scaled up" for control of remote vehicles maneuvering in space, undersea, or on land.[3]

In any of the aforementioned cases of remote manipulation, the remote hand or vehicle, or objects being manipulated, can be virtual (simply computer generated) or real. This suggests that a paradigm like that shown in figure 12.1 can be generalized to an experimental apparatus to explore VR perception.

The discussion of virtual technology research here is provided to help the reader understand how modern technology has truly enabled us to manipulate the perception of what is real. This enables a new kind of behavior research into how humans perceive "where" they are present and what they perceive as reality. The research helps us understand how easily we can be made to experience what is not really there.

There are several "quality" measures that can be applied to virtual environments. One type of measure is the sense of reality—how "immersed" does the human subject feel, measured on a subjective scale. That is important in entertainment applications; however, it may or may not be important in more practical applications, for example, simulation (e.g., flying the flight simulator, performing virtual surgery, checking to make sure the components fit together in a virtual instantiation of a mechanical design or building). In the practical applications cited here, one is concerned with learning, so both performance in the virtual environment and transfer of that learning to the real environment are what is important.

With respect to sense of reality in VR there are three factors that contribute to the experience of reality, the "immersion."

1. The *display information rate*, consisting of the following:

   a. spatial resolution (defined in *pixels* for vision, *taxels* for touch)
   b. temporal resolution (frame refresh rate in images per second)
   c. magnitude resolution (binary bits per pixel embodied in color or gray scale)
   d. Note that the mathematical product of these three quantities (pixels per image, images per second, and bits per pixel) is equal to bits per second, the key metric for rate of information transfer.

2. The *ability to move about* and orient in the sensory space (e.g., to scan a visual display with the eyes, to actively move the hand across a tactile display, to move the body within a virtual room)

3. The *ability of the subject to effect changes* in the virtual environment (e.g., as in remote manipulation)

If what is seen, heard, or touched does not correspond realistically to scanning, viewpoint or bodily changes, the sense of presence is lost. This loss can occur if there is sufficient delay between movement and display response (more than 0.1 second), which can occur if too much computing is necessary to effect timely and accurate movement-to-display transformation.

We have ample evidence that the sense of presence ("immersion") in the virtual environment is enhanced when multiple senses are employed simultaneously (e.g., vision plus hearing, vision plus touch, all three sensory modes). This is in contrast to the subject simply perceiving that he/

she is physically located in a laboratory and simply being asked to play an artificial game. With regard to religion, these same lessons apply to worship rituals. Immersion is amplified by involving all the senses: hearing music or the spoken word, singing, dancing—all while actively imagining the presence of God.

One trick used to enhance the sense of presence is to have the human control, through bodily motions, a human-like avatar (which, in turn, may perform some task in the virtual environment). This is essentially a form of remote manipulation, but the virtual tele-operator is given human-like bodily form. The actual human operator then tends to empathize with the tele-operated avatar.

Finally, there is a mental exercise that has been shown to make a big difference in perception of presence in the virtual environment, and that is for participants to mentally try to *suppress disbelief* (actively resist any tendency to perceive that they are engaging a simulation and not the real thing). Suppression of disbelief is difficult when you are compelled by your senses, where there is feedback consistent with the virtual world and the humans around you play along with the game. This author has participated in such experiments.

Sometimes we speak of divine presence in religious ceremonies. *One has to wonder what there is in common between perception of virtual presence and perception of divine presence.* The reason for wading through the technology and the behavioral research aspects of VR is the suggested connection to understanding belief in the supernatural. *Experience with VR suggests that it is not so difficult to produce a compelling sensation and belief in what is not really there.*

WHAT IS PRESENCE? WHAT IS REALITY?

We conclude from the active development and ready market for VR technology that there is a strong interest by people to engage in VR experiences, perhaps to escape from the somber realities of the real world. VR is enjoyable. Also, we noted two attributes of human behavior that have been shown to enhance the VR experience. The first is that active bodily participation helps to make the virtual seem real. Second, we note that active voluntary suppression of disbelief (that the VR is not real) has a strong effect on enabling psychological "immersion" in the experience. We will have more to say about this later when we discuss the appeal and tendency toward religious belief.

Let us now contrast two ontologies of reality, two philosophical perspectives regarding what is real. One is what is commonly called Cartesian or mind–body dualism—that the brain processes perceptions of the outside world, and these are passed to an immaterial "mind." The latter is attributed to French philosopher René Descartes because he postulated himself as a res cogitans, usually translated as a "thinking substance": He was conscious and existed because he could doubt. But there is controversy as to what he meant was located in the "mind."[4]

Modern science mostly assumes that there is a true material reality "out there" and by means of the scientific method we struggle to bring our scientific and our mental models to be ever closer approximations to the external truths. The brain is surely material and exists. Most scientists do not consider the "mind" to exist apart from the functioning of the brain. There are objective measures of the external environment and subjective measures of what we are thinking. This is called the rationalistic tradition, or realism.

German philosopher Martin Heidegger (1889–1976) rejected the Cartesian view and asserted that all meaning, hence all reality, is conditioned by interpretation, including the beliefs, language, and practices of the interpreter.[5] According to Heidegger, we are thrown into situations where action is unavoidable (*throwness* in Heidegger terminology), the result of such action is unpredictable, and stable representation of the situation is not possible. In normal use of a tool or other object (e.g., in hammering) the tool becomes transparent to the user, who then cannot conceive of the tool independently (it *is ready-to-hand* in Heidegger-speak); however, if some abnormality occurs (e.g., the hammer slips) there *is breakdown*, and the tool can then be conceived in the "mind" (it becomes *present-at-hand*). Normal "being," in Heidegger's view, means complete involvement in a dynamic interaction in which subject and object are inseparable. Only by stepping back and disconnecting from the involvement can a person perceive the separate elements of the situation.

Seemingly related to the Heidegger view are ideas put forth by American psychologist J. J. Gibson. According to Gibson, perception is the acquisition of information that supports action, especially with regard to overcoming constraints on action.[6] Gibson calls this constraint-conformance *affordance*. Actions affect the environment, and the environment in turn affects the action in complete reciprocity. Perceptions are true, as Gibson sees it, to the extent that they support action in the environment.

I find the Heidegger and Gibson views both compatible with one another and credible. The Heidegger–Gibson perspective is credible in the sense that all perception is based on the result of previous action and learning (with the exception of instinctual perception and response). At the same time, there is a credible view that there must be some reality "out there" that forever must be unknown in many (most) respects—no chance to fully unravel it no matter how much science is brought to bear for any finite time into the future. Is that God?

13

METAPHOR, MYTH, AND RELIGIOUS LANGUAGE

RELIGION AS METAPHOR

As stated earlier, metaphor is speech that requires the reader or listener to conjure up in his own mind the meaning, that is, the implied relationship, between the metaphor and a target object or event. A metaphor always has two meanings: a literal one and an implied one.

Read any religious document and you will probably find lots of metaphor. You will find many words and terms that are not explicitly defined. You will have seen many of them from earlier encounters and allow them to pass based on familiarity, having only an imprecise understanding of what the writer really means. It has been said that religious models do not explain but merely evoke a response from the listener. Nietzsche cynically commented that metaphors become accepted and are then regarded as truth.

Is "God" a metaphor? Janet Soskice, a British theologian, writes, "We may justly claim to speak of God without claiming to define Him, and to do so by means of metaphor. Realism accommodates figurative speech, which is reality depicting without claiming to be directly descriptive."[1] Joseph Campbell (1904–1987) claimed,

> God is a metaphor for a mystery that absolutely transcends all human categories of thought, even the categories of being and nonbeing. Those too are categories of thought. I mean it's as simple as that. So it depends on how much you want to think about it, and whether it's

doing you any good. And whether it is putting you in touch with the mystery that's the ground of your own being. If it isn't, well, it's a lie. So half the people in the world are religious people who think that their metaphors are facts. Those are what we call theists. The other half are people who know that the metaphors are not facts. And so, they're lies. Those are the atheists.[2]

RELIGION AS MYTH

A myth is a traditional or legendary story, usually involving some hero or event, with or without a basis of fact or a natural explanation. It is often concerned with deities and explains some practice, rite, or phenomenon of nature.

Campbell is best known for his work in comparative mythology. He claims that myth originates as observations that interact subconsciously with mental projections and are absorbed without criticism. He says that myths put us in touch with the richest dimensions of our lives, even as our inclination is to interpret them literally. He feels that myths must evolve as the world evolves to be relevant to contemporary realities. He claims that myths have four basic functions: (1) the mystical function, experiencing the awe of the universe; (2) the cosmological function, explaining the shape of the universe; (3) the sociological function, supporting and validating social order; and (4) the pedagogical function, how to live as humans.

From all indications, primitive peoples did not make much of a distinction between observed fact and religious myth. Storytelling is how they got their information; there were no newspapers, TV pundits, or fact-checkers. So good stories were what was remembered and passed on. It is often claimed that metaphor originated in mythology. Paul Tillich proposes that all religious language asks to be understood as symbolic and mythical, where a myth is a structure through which a community organizes and make sense of its experience.[3]

GILMAN'S "SACRED FRAGMENTS"

With regard to imagination, I like what Rabbi Neil Gilman has stated about belief, that seeing is not necessarily believing, and that in a mental sense we see what we already believe, what we are prepared to see, what we are convinced we are going to see.[4] This visualization or image-producing of God is not the same as belief in a physical entity. He points out that theological or religious claims do not lend themselves to controlled experimentation and verification, and thus they cannot be disproven in a scientific sense.

In that regard, my philosopher friend, Michael Martin, specialized in atheism and liked to use syllogisms in an effort to disprove the existence of God. I rather enjoyed pointing out to him that in theory, no premise can ever be absolutely disproven, except as stated earlier, within a closed system of symbols like mathematics.

In speaking about God, let us assume that God is myth and that myth is not literally true, but is definitely true in the sense of implication or transcendence, or whatever words you choose to use to try to characterize this mental relationship that we know is beyond denotative natural language. I prefer to expand this realm of God beyond the Buber I-Thou interpersonal relationship and let God stand for all that we do not know and understand, even beyond our daily experience. This I believe moderates the hubris of claiming to know God, and to believe in God as some personal entity. It allows a broader appreciation of our human limitations.

In his popular work *Sacred Fragments*, Gilman emphasizes the importance of myth in thinking about God. He states that since God can be characterized only through metaphor, that is for us precisely what makes him God. We all agree that some religious claims are (otherwise) patently "off-the-wall." Gilman criticizes the Jewish fundamentalist perspective that the Torah is binding in all of its detail. He prefers the so-called naturalist alternative of Rabbi Mordecai Kaplan (1881–1983) that the natural human impulse toward religion manifests itself less through the individual than through human communities and is a discovery by the human mind. God is not a being, certainly not a personal God.[5]

It is like the word "mind" as compared to "brain," where brain refers to an entity. Gilman sees revelation as akin to Martin Buber's *I-Thou* intense interpersonal relation in which two people reveal themselves to one another. Gilman also likes Joshua Heschel's version of God. Heschel emphasizes, as do others, that we can never know God or use human concepts of language to describe God adequately and that the cardinal sin is literal mindedness. That makes the Bible itself a midrash, an interpretation. He claims that no human characterization of God and His activity can be understood as objectively true. Understanding it is through myth, but myths are not capricious inventions. Rather they emerge out of natural experience and promote loyalty to the community. They provide the community with its distinctive raison d'être. The issue is never myth or no myth, but which myth, for myths are the only means available to us for comprehending complex and elusive dimensions of experience.[6]

Gilman distinguishes three pathways to God: (1) reason (the rational approach), (2) experience (the empirical approach), and (3) interpersonal encounter (the existential approach). But for practical purposes, distinguishing religious experience from social encounter is difficult, if not impossible. Most efforts at the rational approach have been dismissed. The champions of the existential approach are Martin Buber and Søren Kierkegaard. Separating the rational from the empirical/existential is sometimes characterized by the difference between "belief that" and "belief in." The latter is characterized by symbols, much as are signs at political rallies or sports contests. Truth means "true for me." The claim is that this makes myth and metaphor different from fiction. Gilman owns up to religious experience being highly subjective. Atheism is tantamount to a failure of perception and failure of will. Seeing nature means seeing God.

Mordecai Kaplan understands religion to be emerging out of the natural functioning of human communities, where God is not a being, but a process.[7] Kaplan uses the analogy of iron filings placed above an electromagnet. The magnetic force is not visible, but the effects on the iron filings are quite apparent. To Kaplan, God is not "beyond nature" in any sense; in fact, there is nothing beyond His nature. So the notion of something that is supernatural is silly. God is a power within nature. We define god by his activity. God is what he does.[8] Kaplan also defines God in terms of human suffering, by posing that God is the total of all the things we discover in our lives.[9] This is the same God that Rabbi Harold Kushner characterizes in his popular 1981 book *Why Bad Things Happen to Good People*.

THE BIBLE AS LITERAL TRUTH

It is common to poke fun at those who take the entire Bible to be literally true. Surely it makes little sense to do so, because much or even most of it is obviously cast in metaphoric language. When the biblical writers moralize we have to realize that the accepted moral and cultural standards at the time those writers lived were very different from what most of us accept as proper standards today.

New atheist writer Sam Harris reminds us that when the fundamentalist's daughter comes home from yoga class and suggests that some respect ought to be given to the teachings of Krishna, she might be reminded of the biblical edict from Deuteronomy 13:7–11:

> If your brother, the son of your father or of your mother, or your son or daughter, or the spouse whom you embrace, or your most intimate friend, tries to secretly seduce you, saying, "Let us go and serve other gods," unknown to you or your ancestors before you, gods of the peoples surrounding you, whether near or far away, anywhere throughout the world, you must not consent, you must not listen to him: You must show him no pity, you must not spare him or conceal his guilt. No, you must kill him, your hands must strike the first blow in putting him to death and the hands of the rest of the people following. You must stone him to death, since he tried to divert you from Yahweh your God. [10]

Harris goes on to point out that much or most of what we hold as sacred based on our religious tradition is not sacred for any reason other than it was thought to be sacred *yesterday*.

With those caveats, the following from Ian Gurvitz paraphrasing Leviticus are cited for the reader's amusement:

Leviticus 1:9 recommends burning a bull on the altar as a sacrifice because it creates a pleasing odor for the Lord.

Leviticus 11:6–8 forbids touching the skin of a dead pig because it makes one unclean (think about footballs, baseball mitts, and leather upholstery).

Leviticus 11:10 prohibits working on the Sabbath (and Exodus 35:2 states that those who do should be put to death).

Leviticus 15:19–24 disallows contact with a woman while she is in her period of menstrual uncleanness.

Leviticus 19:19 warns against planting two different crops in the same field.

Leviticus 19:27 expressly forbids trimming one's hair around the temples.

Leviticus 20:14 indicates that people who sleep with in-laws should be
  burned to death.

Leviticus 21:20 states that one may not approach the altar of God with
  a defect in one's sight.

Leviticus 25:44 states that one may possess slaves, both male and
  female, provided they are purchased from neighboring nations. [11]

Not only the Bible but also many other ancient texts include statements
that now seem strange. Taking such statements as literal guidance for
living today seems rather inappropriate. But metaphor, especially when
considered in the light of history and culture, is a different story. The
following is an example.

YES, VIRGINIA, THERE IS A SANTA CLAUS

On September 21, 1897, the *New York Sun* carried the following now-
famous piece on its editorial page:

> We take pleasure in answering thus prominently the communication
> below, expressing at the same time our great gratification that its faith-
> ful author is numbered among the friends of the *Sun*:
>
> "I am eight years old. Some of my little friends say there is no Santa
> Claus. Papa says, 'If you see it in the *Sun*, it's so.' Please tell me the
> truth, is there a Santa Claus?"
>
> Virginia O'Hanlon
>
> Virginia, your little friends are wrong. They have been affected by the
> skepticism of a skeptical age. They do not believe except what they
> see. They think that nothing can be which is not comprehensible by
> their little minds. All minds, Virginia, whether they be men's or chil-
> dren's, are little. In this great universe of ours, man is a mere insect, an
> ant, in his intellect as compared with the boundless world about him,
> as measured by the Intelligence capable of grasping the whole of truth
> and knowledge.
>
> Yes, Virginia, there is a Santa Claus. He exists as certainly as love
> and generosity and devotion exist, and you know that they abound and
> give to your life its highest beauty and joy. Alas! how dreary would be
> the world if there were no Santa Claus! It would be as dreary as if there
> were no Virginias. There would be no childlike faith then, no poetry,

no romance to make tolerable this existence. We should have no enjoyment, except in sense and sight. The external light with which childhood fills the world would be extinguished.

Not believe in Santa Claus! You might as well not believe in fairies. You might get your papa to hire men to watch in all the chimneys on Christmas Eve to catch Santa Claus, but even if you did not see Santa Claus coming down, what would that prove? Nobody sees Santa Claus, but that is no sign that there is no Santa Claus. The most real things in the world are those that neither children nor men can see. Did you ever see fairies dancing on the lawn? Of course not, but that's no proof that they are not there. Nobody can conceive or imagine all the wonders there are unseen and unseeable in the world.

You tear apart the baby's rattle and see what makes the noise inside, but there is a veil covering the unseen world which not the strongest man, nor even the united strength of all the strongest men that ever lived, could tear apart. Only faith, poetry, love, romance can push aside that curtain and view, and picture the supernal beauty and glory beyond. Is it all real? Ah, Virginia, in all this world there is nothing else real and abiding.

No Santa Claus? Thank God he lives and lives forever. A thousand years from now, Virginia, nay 10 times 10,000 years from now, he will continue to make glad the heart of childhood. Merry Christmas and a Happy New Year!

Here we have a statement that any reader understands to be metaphor and no adult would take literally. Indeed, there is a Santa Claus, and indeed, in a similar metaphorical way, most people would say there is a God. Making the analogy of God to Santa Claus will seem disrespectful to some readers. I do not mean to disrespect the genuine feelings of those readers but only to assert that God makes the most sense as a metaphor for something we feel but cannot define.

14

SPIRITUALITY

The traditional definition of spirituality would refer to religious experience. For example, psychologist William James believed that mental events are attributable to a soul, where each person has a soul that exists in a spiritual universe and leads a person to perform the behaviors they do in the physical world. This was part of what James called *pragmatism*.[1] James defended the right to violate the principle of *evidentialism* (that all belief need be based on evidence and that faith-based belief is unjustified). He sought to ground justified belief in "hypothesis venturing" as an unwavering principle that would prove most beneficial pragmatically. His doctrine allows one to assume belief in God and prove His existence by what the belief brings to one's life. Justifying belief based on what makes one feel good and makes one's life richer is an interesting argument. It might also be noted that sometimes the truth hurts, so why not engage in pleasurable thoughts?

According to the Dalai Lama, a broad definition of spirituality includes a much wider swath of experiences, for instance, love, compassion, patience, tolerance, forgiveness, contentment, responsibility, harmony, inner peace, and a concern for others.[2] These are aspects of life and human experience that clearly go beyond a purely materialist view of the world, without demanding belief in a supernatural reality or divine being. Spirituality embodies a sense of interdependence of everything and harmony in the universe. Feelings of awe and wonder about where we came from, how we got here, where we are going, what is the purpose of life, etc., can be called spiritual and independent of religion, at least in the

sense of belief in any God. It can be said that everyone, atheist or believer, has times of having what can be called a spiritual experience. Spirituality has been associated with not only what is sacred (worthy of venera-
tion), but also substance abuse (getting high), near-death events, par-
ent–child relationships, and ecological fervor. Meditation, transcendental
or otherwise, is said to be spiritual.

Spirituality is a feeling, an experience, that defies explication in literal
terms. Spirituality, whether in respect to people or other aspects of nature,
is hard to talk about if the words are intended as denotative (precise
specifications with uniformly understood meanings). Mostly by using
metaphor we can use words that surely communicate. Doing psychophysics, that is, the study of mental experience as a function of the physical
properties of external stimuli (like a hearing or vision test), we would not
call a spiritual exercise. In contrast, listening to music is clearly spiritual.
Many of the great works of music are spiritual and may be religiously
inspired. Who is not thrilled by Beethoven's *Ode to Joy* or Handel's
Messiah, or by the booming organs in the great European cathedrals? One
can easily assert that the atheist can just as easily be thrilled by such
music. Spirituality corresponds to the enjoyment of nature on almost any
physical scale. The more catholic (!) meaning of spirituality is secular.

Seemingly falling in line with our ancient ancestors, people often
attribute spiritual qualities to people who are our heroes. Not only Jesus,
Moses, and Mohammed qualify, but also, depending on who and when,
Kennedy, Hitler, Elvis, and Batman qualify. We like kings and queens,
and if they don't exist for us in real life, we invent them in our literature
and media. Even in the United States, founded on the basis that democratic people owe allegiance to no worldly king or dictator, we post photos of
our president and other national leaders in the entrances of our public
buildings, just as do monarchies and communist bureaucracies. Much of
the public loved Ronald Reagan, who many pundits admitted made a
better American king than a president. They disliked Jimmy Carter because his appearance and manner did not convey a sense of royalty. In
this regard, it is worth recalling the amazing outpouring of grief and
affection for Diana, Princess of Wales, upon her untimely death. What
was it about this woman, born into a wealthy, if dysfunctional, family,
married to a less-than-exciting English prince, chased by the paparazzi
and pictured in the tabloids, that elicited such a response? Clearly the
public of Britain wanted someone they could place on a pedestal who also

had the spiritual qualities of beauty and mystery. Spirituality in this sense is natural but can also be delusory.

Physicist/novelist Alan Lightman professes to be an atheist. But in his book *The Accidental Universe* he poignantly describes an encounter which he claims to be truly spiritual, and transcendent.[3] He had been observing an osprey nest for weeks from his back porch, and he felt the osprey adolescents had been observing him in return. One day two of them took flight and dove directly at him, coming eye to eye with him before they zoomed upward. He found himself shaking and in tears as a result. In another book he describes how he felt when lying on his back looking at the stars while summering on an island off the coast of Maine:

> For me as both a scientist and a humanist, the transcendent experience is the most powerful evidence we have for a spiritual world. For this I mean the immediate and vital personal experience of being connected to something larger than ourselves, to seeing some unseen order or truth in the world.[4]

15

OPPOSING PERSPECTIVES THAT SEEM TO CONVERGE

In September 2009, the *Wall Street Journal* commissioned Oxford historian of religion Karen Armstrong (1944–) and British evolutionist Richard Dawkins to respond independently to the question, "Where does evolution leave God?" Armstrong is a well-regarded author of many popular books on the history of religion and a champion of God. Dawkins is probably the most widely read champion of new atheism. Neither knew what the other would say. Here are the results. The exchange is quoted in full because in my opinion it shows how close a respected religious apologist and a devout atheist can become.

Karen Armstrong Says We Need God to Grasp the Wonder of Our Existence

Richard Dawkins has been right all along, of course—at least in one important respect. Evolution has indeed dealt a blow to the idea of a benign creator, literally conceived. It tells us that there is no Intelligence controlling the cosmos and that life itself is the result of a blind process of natural selection, in which innumerable species failed to survive.

The fossil record reveals a natural history of pain, death, and racial extinction, so if there was a divine plan, it was cruel, callously prodigal, and wasteful. Human beings were not the pinnacle of a purposeful creation; like everything else, they evolved by trial and error, and God had no direct hand in their making. No wonder so many fundamentalist Christians find their faith shaken to the core.

But Darwin may have done religion—and God—a favor by reveal-
ing a flaw in modern Western faith. Despite our scientific and technological brilliance, our understanding of God is often remarkably unde-
veloped—even primitive. In the past, many of the most influential
Jewish, Christian, and Muslim thinkers understood that *what we call
"God" is merely a symbol that points beyond itself to an indescribable
transcendence, whose existence cannot be proved but is only intuited
by means of spiritual exercises and a compassionate lifestyle that enables us to cultivate new capacities of mind and heart.*

But by the end of the seventeenth century, instead of looking
through the symbol to "the God beyond God," Christians were trans-
forming it into hard fact. Sir Isaac Newton had claimed that his cosmic
system proved beyond doubt the existence of an intelligent, omniscient, and omnipotent creator, who was obviously "very well skilled
in Mechanicks and Geometry." Enthralled by the prospect of such
cast-iron certainty, churchmen started to develop a scientifically based
theology that eventually made Newton's Mechanick, and later William
Paley's Intelligent Designer, essential to Western Christianity.

But the Great Mechanick was little more than an idol, the kind of
human projection that theology, at its best, was supposed to avoid.
God had been essential to Newtonian physics, but it was not long
before other scientists were able to dispense with the God-hypothesis,
and, finally, Darwin showed that there could be no proof for God's
existence. This would not have been a disaster had not Christians
become so dependent upon their scientific religion that they had lost
the older habits of thought and were left without other resources.

Symbolism was essential to premodern religion, because it was
only possible to speak about the ultimate reality—God, Tao, Brahman,
or Nirvana—analogically, since it lay beyond the reach of words. Jews
and Christians both developed audaciously innovative and figurative
methods of reading the Bible, and every statement of the Quran is
called an ayah (parable). Saint Augustine, a major authority for both
Catholics and Protestants, insisted that if a biblical text contradicted
reputable science, it must be interpreted allegorically. This remained
standard practice in the West until the seventeenth century, when, in an
effort to emulate the exact scientific method, Christians began to read
scripture with a literalness that is without parallel in religious history.

Most cultures believed that there were two recognized ways of
arriving at truth. The Greeks called them *mythos* and *logos*. Both were
essential, and neither was superior to the other; they were not in conflict, but complementary, each with its own sphere of competence.

Logos ("reason") was the pragmatic mode of thought that enabled us to function effectively in the world and had, therefore, to correspond accurately to external reality. But it could not assuage human grief or find ultimate meaning in life's struggle. For that people turned to mythos, stories that made no pretensions to historical accuracy but should rather be seen as an early form of psychology. If translated into ritual or ethical action, *a good myth showed you how to cope with mortality, discover an inner source of strength, and endure pain and sorrow with serenity.*

In the ancient world, a cosmology was not regarded as factual, but was primarily therapeutic; it was recited when people needed an infusion of that mysterious power that had somehow brought something out of primal nothingness: at a sickbed, a coronation, or during a political crisis. Some cosmologies taught people how to unlock their own creativity; others made them aware of the struggle required to maintain social and political order. The Genesis creation hymn, written during the Israelites' exile in Babylonia in the sixth century BC, was a gentle polemic against Babylonian religion. Its vision of an ordered universe where everything had its place was probably consoling to a displaced people, though, as we can see in the Bible, some of the exiles preferred a more aggressive cosmology.

There can never be a definitive version of a myth, because it refers to the more imponderable aspects of life. To remain effective, it must respond to contemporary circumstance. In the sixteenth century, when Jews were being expelled from one region of Europe after another, the mystic Isaac Luria constructed an entirely new creation myth that bore no resemblance to the Genesis story. But instead of being reviled for contradicting the Bible, it inspired a mass movement among Jews, because it was such a telling description of the arbitrary world they now lived in. Backed up with special rituals, it also helped them face up to their pain and discover a source of strength.

Religion was not supposed to provide explanations that lay within the competence of reason, but to help us live creatively with realities for which there are no easy solutions and find an interior haven of peace; today, however, many have opted for unsustainable certainty instead. But can we respond religiously to evolutionary theory? Can we use it to recover a more authentic notion of God?

Darwin made it clear that—as Maimonides, Aquinas, and Eckhart had already pointed out—we cannot regard God simply as a divine personality who single-handedly created the world. This could direct our attention away from the idols of certainty and back to the "God beyond God." The best theology is a spiritual exercise, akin to poetry. *Religion is not an exact science but a kind of art form that, like music or painting, introduces us to a mode of knowledge that is different from the purely rational and which cannot easily be put into words* . At its best, it holds us in an attitude of wonder, which is, perhaps, not unlike the awe that Mr. Dawkins experiences—and has helped me to appreciate—when he contemplates the marvels of natural selection.

But what of the pain and waste that Darwin unveiled? All the major traditions insist that the faithful meditate on the ubiquitous suffering that is an inescapable part of life; because, if we do not acknowledge this uncomfortable fact, the compassion that lies at the heart of faith is impossible. The almost unbearable spectacle of the myriad species passing painfully into oblivion is not unlike some classic Buddhist meditations on the First Noble Truth ("Existence is suffering"), the indispensable prerequisite for the transcendent enlightenment that some call Nirvana—and others call God. [1]

Richard Dawkins Argues That Evolution
Leaves God with Nothing to Do

Before 1859, it would have seemed natural to agree with the Reverend William Paley, in *Natural Theology*, that the creation of life was God's greatest work. Especially (vanity might add) human life. Today we might amend the statement: Evolution is the universe's greatest work. Evolution is the creator of life, and life is arguably the most surprising and most beautiful production that the laws of physics have ever generated. Evolution, to quote a T-shirt sent to me by an anonymous well-wisher, is the greatest show on earth, the only game in town.

Indeed, evolution is probably the greatest show in the entire universe. Most scientists' hunch is that there are independently evolved life forms dotted around planetary islands throughout the universe—though sadly too thinly scattered to encounter one another. And if there is life elsewhere, it is something stronger than a hunch to say that it will turn out to be Darwinian life. The argument in favor of alien life's existing at all is weaker than the argument that—if it exists at all—it will be Darwinian life. But it is also possible that we really are alone in the universe, in which case Earth, with its greatest show, is the most remarkable planet in the universe.

What is so special about life? It never violates the laws of physics. Nothing does (if anything did, physicists would just have to formulate new laws—it's happened often enough in the history of science). But although life never violates the laws of physics, it pushes them into unexpected avenues that stagger the imagination. If we didn't know about life we wouldn't believe it was possible—except, of course, that there'd then be nobody around to do the disbelieving!

The laws of physics, before Darwinian evolution bursts out from their midst, can make rocks and sand, gas clouds and stars, whirlpools and waves, whirlpool-shaped galaxies and light that travels as waves while behaving like particles. It is an interesting, fascinating, and, in many ways, deeply mysterious universe. But now, enter life. Look, through the eyes of a physicist, at a bounding kangaroo, a swooping bat, a leaping dolphin, a soaring coast redwood. There never was a rock that bounded like a kangaroo, never a pebble that crawled like a beetle seeking a mate, never a sand grain that swam like a water flea. Not once do any of these creatures disobey one jot or tittle of the laws of physics. Far from violating the laws of thermodynamics (as is often ignorantly alleged) they are relentlessly driven by them. Far from violating the laws of motion, animals exploit them to their advantage as they walk, run, dodge and jink, leap and fly, pounce on prey or spring to safety.

Never once are the laws of physics violated, yet life emerges into uncharted territory. And how is the trick done? The answer is a process that, although variable in its wondrous detail, is sufficiently uniform to deserve one single name: Darwinian evolution, the nonrandom survival of randomly varying coded information. We know, as certainly as we know anything in science, that this is the process that has generated life on our own planet. And my bet, as I said, is that the same process is in operation wherever life may be found, anywhere in the universe.

What if the greatest show on earth is not the greatest show in the universe? What if there are life forms on other planets that have evolved so far beyond our level of intelligence and creativity that we should regard them as Gods, were we ever so fortunate (or unfortunate?) as to meet them? Would they indeed be Gods? Wouldn't we be tempted to fall on our knees and worship them, as a medieval peasant might if suddenly confronted with such miracles as a Boeing 747, a mobile telephone, or Google Earth? But, however God-like the aliens might seem, they would not be Gods, and for one very important reason. They did not create the universe; it created them, just as it created us. Making the universe is the one thing no intelligence, however superhuman, could do, because an intelligence is complex—statistically improbable—and therefore had to emerge, by gradual degrees, from simpler beginnings: from a lifeless universe the miracle-free zone that is physics.

To midwife such emergence is the singular achievement of Darwinian evolution. It starts with primeval simplicity and fosters, by slow, explicable degrees, the emergence of complexity: seemingly limitless complexity—certainly up to our human level of complexity and very probably way beyond. There may be worlds on which superhuman life thrives, superhuman to a level that our imaginations cannot grasp. But superhuman does not mean supernatural. Darwinian evolution is the only process we know that is ultimately capable of generating anything as complicated as creative intelligences. Once it has done so, of course, those intelligences can create other complex things: works of art and music, advanced technology, computers, the internet, and who knows what in the future? Darwinian evolution may not be the only such generative process in the universe.

There may be other "cranes" (Daniel Dennett's term, which he opposes to "skyhooks") that we have not yet discovered or imagined. But, however wonderful and however different from Darwinian evolution those putative cranes may be, they cannot be magic. They will share with Darwinian evolution the facility to raise up complexity, as an emergent property, out of simplicity, while never violating natural law.

Where does that leave God? The kindest thing to say is that it leaves him with nothing to do, and no achievements that might attract our praise, our worship, or our fear. Evolution is God's redundancy notice, his pink slip. But we have to go further. A complex creative intelligence with nothing to do is not just redundant. A divine designer is all but ruled out by the consideration that he must be at least as complex as the entities he was wheeled out to explain. God is not dead. He was never alive in the first place.

Now, there is a certain class of sophisticated modern theologians who will say something like this: "Good heavens, of course we are not so naive or simplistic as to care whether God exists. Existence is such a nineteenth-century preoccupation! It doesn't matter whether God exists in a scientific sense. What matters is whether he exists for you or for me. If God is real for you, who cares whether science has made him redundant? Such arrogance! Such elitism."

Well, if that's what floats your canoe, you'll be paddling it up a very lonely creek. The mainstream belief of the world's peoples is very clear. They believe in God, and that means they believe he exists in objective reality, just as surely as the Rock of Gibraltar exists. If sophisticated theologians or postmodern relativists think they are rescuing God from the redundancy scrap heap by downplaying the importance of existence, they should think again. Tell the congregation of a church or mosque that existence is too vulgar an attribute to fasten onto their God, and they will brand you an atheist. They'll be right.[2]

CONVERGENCE? TRANSCENDENCE?

What so impresses me about this exchange is that Armstrong and Dawkins, who the *Wall Street Journal* quite naturally assumed would take polar opposite positions, ended up close to the same place. Armstrong emphasizes that modern science has rendered fundamentalist literalist notions of God as untenable to science and a rational person, while claiming that science has failed to cope with human consciousness and sense of transcendent reality. She refers to religion as a spiritual exercise but certain belief as untenable. I believe this is what R. Buckminster Fuller meant by the quote I put at the beginning of this chapter: "God is a verb."

And Dawkins is certainly correct that "even modern theology, if it looks itself in the mirror, has moved in the atheist direction," to a large extent. Surely modern technology, as viewed by a primitive observer, would be attributed to God. But most of the world, modern philosophy notwithstanding, is still mired in that past—and that's our problem.

What is transcendence? Is it another term for "I don't know and I don't understand"?

Does God really have anything useful to do? Is the mythos aspect of Karen Armstrong's argument that we can treat myth the same as we do Santa Claus, or is it some transcendent myth that is a clear guideline for living?

British philosopher Alfred J. Ayer (1910–1989) took a much more cynical view of talking about God as transcendent.[3] He commented that to say that something transcends human understanding is to say that it is unintelligible, and what is unintelligible cannot be significantly described. He claimed that one cannot intelligibly believe in God unless one can give an account of what it means to say God exists. If one allows that it is impossible to define God in intelligible terms, then one is allowing that it is impossible for a sentence to be both significant and be about God. To assert that words are inadequate and approximate does not help, for, because words have only the meanings we give them, if we cannot say what we mean, we cannot genuinely claim to mean anything. No sentence which purports to describe the nature of a transcendent God can possess any literal significance.

Contemporary British philosopher of religion Don Cupitt (1934–) allegedly started from a position that human language could never fully express the reality of God.[4] He then evolved to embracing the notion that God is not a being who exists independently of us, but is instead a product of our language and ideas. This can be restated: God did not create us in God's image; we created God in our image. That is not a new idea, but it is an important one, and I will pick up on it later. Cupitt, by the way, sees Jesus as a radical secular humanist.

16

QUESTIONS ABOUT CHURCHGOERS

WHY DO PEOPLE AFFILIATE WITH ONLY ONE RELIGIOUS TRIBE?

People tend to regard religious institutions in much the same way as they do athletic teams: They tend to become fans of one team or another. One is expected to identify a religious preference one way or another. When this author did his service during the Korean War, his dog tags had to say Catholic, Protestant, or Jew. There was no alternative. The following makes the point. It is an exchange between a young Indian boy and his parents in Yann Martel's novel *Life of Pi*.

> "But I want to pray to Allah. I want to be a Christian."
> "You can't be both. You must be one or the other."
> "Why can't I be both?"
> "They're separate religions. They have nothing in common."
> "That's not what they say! They both claim Abraham as theirs. Muslims say the God of the Hebrews and the Christians is the same as the God of the Muslims. They recognize David, Moses, and Jesus as prophets."
> "What does this have to do with us, Piscine? We're Indians."
> "There have been Christians and Muslims in India for centuries. Some people say Jesus is buried in Kashmir."
> He said nothing, only looked at me, his brow furrowed. Suddenly business called.
> "Talk to Mother about it."
> "Mother."

"Father and I find your religious zeal a bit of a mystery."

"It is a mystery."

"Hmmmm. I don't mean it that way. Listen, my darling, if you're going to be religious, you must be either a Hindu, a Christian, or a Muslim. You heard what they said on the esplanade."

"I don't see why I can't be all three." [1]

Society tends to force us to choose between religions, to join one tribe or another. Why should not each person consider them all and synthesize his or her own religion? Actually, some religious institutions do try to do this. One is the Bahai faith, which explicitly seeks to combine the best from Christianity, Islam, and Buddhism. Another is the Unitarian Universalist Society, which welcomes atheists, as well as all shades of believers.

PRAYER: DOES IT WORK?

Looking back in history there are good reasons why certain religious practices, for instance, prayer, developed as they did. Ancient peoples built altars on which they sacrificed living creatures, including children, because they honestly thought that would win them favor with the gods.

Prayer is a prominent component of essentially all religious practice. Asking favors of God or the gods though prayer has been standard for thousands of years. Intercessory prayer, praying for others, is admirable caring. But a salient question is whether intercessory prayer really works, whether those prayed for become better off. Various scientific studies have been conducted ever since Francis Galton first addressed it in 1872. [2] But little credible evidence has become available that shows that prayer influences the probability that the request will come true.

C. S. Lewis (1898–1963), writing on the efficacy of prayer, comments disparagingly about "those artificially contrived experiences which we call experiments." He continues, "Could this be done about prayer? I will pass over the objection that no Christian could take part in such a project, because He has been forbidden it: You must not try experiments on God, your Master." Lewis goes on to suggest that people praying in an experiment would not really be praying but only mouthing the words. Quoting Hamlet, he asserts, "Words without thoughts never to heaven go." [3]

Actually, many experimental studies on prayer have already been done. The great majority show no significant effect. One can find on the internet reports of double-blind experiments that purport to show with statistical significance that medical patients have better outcomes if patients are prayed for; however, most of those studies were supported by religious organizations and are therefore suspect as being biased. If patients are informed or otherwise get wind of the fact that they are being prayed for there is an obvious opportunity for a placebo effect, well established in behavioral science. So, let someone know you are praying for them, and an effect cannot be disputed.

Eric Stockton, agreeing with Lewis that experiments are not possible (but with a different perspective), comments, "Of course, there is a question whether a true test of prayer is even possible." He points out in a letter to the editor of *Skeptical Inquirer*,

> If prayer works because of God's intervention, and God is the omniscient deity of Christianity (or most any major religion), then He knows He is being tested. As such, He could accept or reject whatever prayer is offered and either choose to give or not give evidence that it works. It would be impossible to properly blind such an experiment if it's the deity we're talking about. If it is supposed to be the prayer itself that heals, rather than God intervening, then we don't have that issue, but we instead have to wonder how it might be that such prayer might work, if we ever get a decent study that shows it does, that is. [4]

In many religions, including Christianity, one purpose of prayer is not to ask for things to happen, but to praise and honor God, and develop a personal relation. This, in turn, raises the question of what that means if God is transcendent and intangible. Since that God must be imagined (there can be no other way of making contact), is that any different from one obtaining satisfaction from identifying with any other personal hero, say a famous movie personality or athletic superstar? And then if that is what is going on and the person obtains satisfaction from such a personal relationship, is there anything unusual in that? We all enjoy our heroes, whether in business, sports, personal relations, or religion.

DOES RELIGIOUS PRACTICE ENHANCE HEALTH?

There is growing evidence from epidemiological data, clinical trials, and cross-sectional studies of a positive correlation between religious practice and health. These studies appear in peer-reviewed journals; have been reported by different research groups; and have been replicated for people of all ages, races, and socioeconomic strata. For example, the Women's Health Initiative, through surveys and an annual review of medical records, found that women older than 50 were 20 percent less likely to die in any given year if they attended religious services weekly (15 percent reduction if they attended less than weekly) compared to those that never attend religious services.[5] This analysis was controlled for age, ethnicity, income level, and, most importantly, current health status; however, concern remains that perhaps religious people are either more likely to be mentally healthy in the first place (based on personality or genetic influences) or that uncontrolled factors are responsible for these associations.

These findings raise the interesting question of whether it is rational for people to practice religion and express belief in God because that makes them feel good. Is belief in any untruth ever justified, for example, if it generates happiness? The answer would seem to be yes, provisionally. If no one is harmed and belief (in a hypothetical untruth) makes the believer happy, it is hard to assert that such a person should be denied that good feeling. Of course, believers might contend that God really does help them and that it is more than a psychological effect of their effort to believe or their commitment in belief. (I remind the reader that, as discussed earlier, effort to believe in a technologically produced virtual environment does make it seem more real, even though it is contrived.)

It can be said that no current understanding of anything is completely true (science is continually refining the truth). I think that many professed believers justify their belief this way. I can only suggest that there is satisfaction if one aspires to be intellectually honest and actively seek truth.

DO RELIGIOUS INSTITUTIONS DO MORE GOOD THAN HARM?

I find this a difficult question to answer. Globally we see that the clash between the values of Western Christianity and Middle Eastern Islam, played out in the media and in international politics, are precipitating global conflict. The ancient rivalries based on who should have succeeded the Prophet Mohammed many centuries ago or who is responsible for killing Jesus appear infantile. And it is the innocent people who suffer.

At the local level, however, within small communities where tribal values are held in common, we see that religious institutions perform many good deeds. They comfort the sick and lonely, and promote good causes. African American churches were clearly instrumental in the civil rights movement in the United States. Religious institutions provide a sense of community that government agencies are unable to do. The sense of community is mostly a good thing, but sometimes it manifests peer pressure and tribal reinforcement for people to take up causes that are not very admirable. So, a question that emerges is this: Can institutions that revolve around commitment but are not religious produce similar benefits without the costs?

DO CHURCHGOERS SAY WHAT THEY REALLY BELIEVE?

Having sat with a small sample of churchgoers in discussions about God during a period of many years, this writer's opinion is that it is very uncomfortable for most people to talk about God openly. My sample may be biased; it surely is biased in one way or another. The subject of God is intellectually intimidating for many. At least in Western cultures many folks are just not comfortable sharing their true religious beliefs, because often those beliefs are not well articulated in peoples' own minds. Most folks who were brought up to attend church or say they profess one faith or another will continue to follow their habits and traditions, "believing in believing" as Dennett so aptly puts it, and do not want to rock the boat. For this reason, getting directly at religious belief through scientific methods is a tricky but challenging pursuit.

Readers may remember that just before Christmas 2012, there was a horrific massacre of 20 first grade children and seven teachers in Newtown, Connecticut. This was but one of hundreds of handgun killings by deranged youth in the United States in recent years. My wife and I watched the moving memorial service on TV. Clergy from many faith traditions, including Roman Catholic, Jewish, Muslim, Bahai, and multiple flavors of Protestant Christians, offered prayers in a wonderful display of togetherness. President Obama spoke and also emphasized the coming together. The Muslims commented on the "artificial divisions" between faith traditions. (I agree, why do we perpetuate, even celebrate these divisions?) One of the clergy commented that the victims are now in a "better place." (Better place? If death is better, then why the sadness?) The service was moving precisely because of the human mutual caring, not because God contributed very much. He appeared to be absent as the children were being murdered. But many believers persist in affirming God's love and feeling that somehow such heinous crimes are part of His plan.

RELIGIOUS PRACTICES ARE CULTURE, AND CHANGING CULTURE IS NOT EASY FOR THE BRAIN

Understanding religion in a scientific way is hardly a new idea, and it is totally naïve to think that it can be done easily. Religion is deeply embedded in human culture. But that is no excuse for not putting effort into new thinking and new models.

In an interview at the Berkeley Institute of International Studies in 2000, a late friend of mine, professor and neurologist Lawrence Stark, had some interesting comments about mental models and God:

> So much of our interaction is within our own brains, and the contact we have with other people and with the outside world is very sparse. People can have a model in their head and that model subsumes their thinking process, and it's almost impossible to change that model. So one can have a model of a gray-haired God up in the sky, and if you believe that, then everything that happens is a result of that person watching over you and doing this and doing that. Once you have that model, it's very hard to shake the model. Each brain cell in our cortex has about 20,000 connections, 10,000 to other cells and 10,000 from other cells. And of those 10,000 inputs and outputs to each cell in the cerebral cortex, only one of them goes to the outside world, for example, to move a muscle. Only one of them, on average, comes from the outside world, for example, to carry a vision signal or a temperature signal. These billions of neurons are all talking to each other through all these connections, and they're only getting sparse information from the outside. So the generation of models in people's heads and the functioning of those models are what drives them. I think that's one of the real problems in humanity, that people can't really interact, and the way they form their models is shaped by very primitive forces in our

culture, and in every culture. I think people who want to change the world are going to have to change the models.[6]

EVOLUTION OF THE CHURCH

No one can scoff at the sheer number of church/synagogue/temple/ mosque organizations, buildings, and effective outreach. Looking into the future, what is the proper role for church organizations? Church organizations are marvelous vehicles for encouraging mutual caring both within and outside of their congregations. Caring for one another in the local community, as well as the world community, is not inconsistent with tenets of all the world religions. There is no need to reject organizations serving that important need, which local and state governments do not and cannot provide.

To accomplish these objectives why do we need the supernatural religion component? We call the religious institutions faith communities, but is the faith (presumably faith in a supernatural God and faith in the sacred texts) really necessary to the community part? Is the purpose of the religious component to engender fear—that if we do not love our neighbors God will send us to hell? If we do not believe, is there a chance that we are forever condemned, so that according to Pascal's wager it would be wiser to believe and not risk even a small chance of eternal damnation? If we do not at least act like we believe, will we be ostracized from the tribe? I suspect some people really do accept those justifications for "belief" (however insincere).

There are other motives to question religion. Religion as a basis for morality is being questioned in the public square as never before, for instance, by Sam Harris, as previously mentioned. With regard to faith, how about faith in morality derived from pragmatic experience? Instead of religious faith, how about engendering faith in one another? A community organization devoted to building faith in one another and spreading that into the community and the world would seem to be a good thing.

It is easy to imagine the kind of secular congregation meeting I'm talking about. We need not dispense with a choir and music, even traditional sacred music. Sacred music is part of our culture and is common in many otherwise secular music venues. In the revised "churches" there could be talks by folks selected by a governance committee or panel discussions. There could be organizational activities of various kinds, committee reports, activities for children—pretty much all the same activities as at present with the exception of liturgy. Prayer to God could be replaced by contemplative exercises designed to enhance appreciation for the beauty and the wonders that surround us. Religious education could be replaced by moral/ethical education. No problem meeting in the (former) church buildings.

Actually, some church congregations have been moving in these directions for years. Probably the Unitarian Universalist Society is furthest along. Then there are such groups as the Bahai, who selectively draw inspiration from just about all the world's religions. Unfortunately, both groups are marginalized by "true believers" in the larger religions.

Of course, much of what I applaud in the aforementioned paragraphs is already being pushed by organizations that call themselves secular humanists. There exist various organizations that promote secular humanism. They have also been known as just humanists, freethinkers, ethical culturists, and "brights" (Dennett's proposed term,[7] which this writer finds repugnant). Auguste Comte (1798–1857), founder of positivist philosophy, attempted to produce a religion of humanity in France in 1851.[8] A humanist manifesto was created at the University of Chicago in 1933.[9] The International Humanist and Ethical Union was founded in 1952, when a gathering of world humanists met under the leadership of Julian Huxley. The American Humanist Association, founded in 1941, has many associated groups, for example, the Council for Secular Humanism. The International Humanist and Ethical Union (IHEU) is the world union of more than 100 humanist, rationalist, irreligious, atheist, ethical culture, and free-thought organizations in more than 40 countries. So, the idea of secular humanism is certainly not new. I suspect that those whose health is currently sustained by attending religious services would fare just as well in meetings of the secular humanist organization. The togetherness and the mutual caring, and the good works, would still be there.

17

REDEFINING GOD,
GOD BY OTHER NAMES

CREATING GOD IN OUR OWN IMAGE?

Abrahamic religions promote the idea that humans are "created by God in His own image," at least that's what Genesis says about Adam and Eve. This statement applies to meanings of "image" that are not restricted to a visual image: love, forgiveness, etc. In any case, the "image" of today's human that God is said to have created is not always admirable. Most folks are more hateful, ignorant, fatter, and less than ideal in many other ways: Is that the image of God they want to present?

What seems more obvious is what Don Cupitt[1] and others have said: We humans create God in our own image. For many it's an old man in the sky looking down and smiling on all of us, or ready to punish us if we don't toe the line. Usually it's some kind of anthropomorphic entity capable of caring about each and every one of us. Does that include all animals, bacteria, plants, and living cells (and all subatomic particles in the universe?!). God is regarded as an ideal person: all-loving, all-knowing, all-powerful. The trouble is, there is nothing we can observe, so no real "image" available, except what we may imagine.

A LIBERAL JEWISH "PLAUSIBLE GOD"

Philosopher Mitchell Silver analyzes the theology of three contemporary Jewish philosophers, Mordechai Kaplan, Michael Lerner, and Arthur Green, in terms of what he posits as a dichotomy between an "Old supernatural God" and a "New God."[2] The New God is seemingly aligned with Spinoza's "one substance" God, comprising the entirety of nature, and having no separate parts and no personal attributes like will, interest, or desires.

Silver characterizes the New God as potential energy for goodness and self-consciousness, a "value motivator," and "whatever there is in nature that makes good things possible."[3] He claims that the New God is also a name for wonder. Theism, from this new perspective, is equivalent to optimism, while atheism, from his perspective, equates to pessimism. Where purely natural laws operate without judge or judgment, the New God perspective is seen as a basis for a world that returns good for good, and evil for evil.

The New God, Silver claims, is more a celebration of life and self than the Pauline denial of this world. The New God's divinity is more like beauty than truth, and joy in the mysteries of existence than the traditional characterization of God as a supernatural omnipotent omniscient person. Religious truth is thus an aesthetic claim and "does not speak to the factual nature of reality." The job of God language, then, is not to produce belief, but rather to motivate "so as to produce affect and effect."[4]

Where the terms "secular" and "humanism" are commonly used together, Silver makes a distinction, noting that pure secularism denies any kind of God. Secularism is naturalism plus atheism, whereas humanism can accommodate the New God. He speaks of God as a heuristic for prayer and defines contemplative prayer as reverential active appreciation of life and our universe. This is not contemplation of propositions regarding truth, but rather a contemplation of images that create experiential value. He asserts that God only exists where He is imagined, and so serves to name the mystical experience and its cause.

Because Silver's New God is expressed in terms of imagination, mysticism, aesthetics, optimism, and human values, that description can be said to be the epitome of connotation. It is still not close to anything that can be modeled denotatively, although it is quite different from the supernatural Old God. It is decidedly close to the message of this book, that respectful humanism, and respect for the natural wonders of our world, are what are important. I have no objection to the term "secular humanism," provided that it embodies the kind of reverence so nicely expressed in a book by Paul Woodruff, entitled *Reverence*, which is discussed in the next chapter. I do not believe that atheism need have a negative connotation, as Silver implies, if it means disbelief in a supernatural God.

A BETTER DEFINITION OF GOD (REVISITING GOD OF THE GAPS)

Recall Joseph Campbell's definition that, "God is a metaphor for a mystery that absolutely transcends all human categories of thought." And recall the notion of "God of the gaps," the usually pejorative term for filling holes in our lack of knowledge with a supernatural agent. The God of the gaps term has been used historically as a derogatory term against those who do not believe fully in the traditional supernatural God.

But let us reconsider whether filling those holes in our knowledge and understanding with a supernatural entity is appropriate. Why not fill the holes with honest admission that we don't know and don't understand so much of what we experience? Most such gaps we will never be able to fill. We can easily go along with Campbell and retain the word "God," as traditionally used, in the metaphor category. But why not at the same time adopt the term "God" to refer to all that is mystery—without any connotation of a supernatural God? I rather think that many modern churchgoers, when they stop to think about it, place their belief squarely there but are reluctant to admit that.

Scientists can seem arrogant, as many critics of the new atheism are fond to point out. Science does not have all the answers. Indeed, built into the scientific methodology is robust effort to disprove whatever "facts" currently prevail. Unfortunately, the public typically does not appreciate this point.

There is so much we do not know and understand. Humility is healthy in this regard, and we need more of it in facing the big questions about who we are and where we came from. But that certainly does not mean that we abandon intellectual honesty and rationality by substituting the easy answer that God did it. The universe is full of wonders, mysteries we do not and surely will not ever understand. God can happily serve as shorthand for respect and awe for those aspects of life that are clearly beyond our grasp. Such a God (we don't need to call it that) is a wonderful antidote for the hubris of asserting that our God is better than someone else's God. That New God, the God of experiencing awe, appreciation, acceptance, and humility before the mystery and vastness of nature and the universe, in no way accedes to supernaturalism.

Part IV

Respecting Others

18

RESPECTING OTHERS' BELIEFS VERSUS RESPECTING OTHERS' HUMANITY

This chapter tackles the issues raised in the introduction, that modern atheism is seen to be disrespectful of others' beliefs, why that is so, whether it is deserved, and how the atheist should respond. Furthermore, there is the historical fact that atheists are often disrespected. Is it just because they are *disrepectful* of others? Atheists want to be respected as human beings. And naturally those with other beliefs want to be respected as human beings. Maybe greater *mutual respect* is called for.

Respect for others means many things. It seems to include compassion, morality, and even reverence (in a secular sense, to be explained). It also includes a degree of trust, trust in others as humans with a right to their beliefs, not necessarily trust in the correctness of those beliefs per se. Developing trust is a challenge based to a great extent on the mutuality of the trusting relationship, as is illustrated here by the game of "prisoner's dilemma." What religious traditions call *faith* has a strong connection to trust.

After reviewing these concepts, the chapter ends with a brief discussion of how awareness of one's ignorance motivates one to seek understanding of the other and the delicate "trade-offs" in being honest with one's conscience in standing up for one's beliefs, while at the same time respecting other people who hold differing beliefs.

What does it mean to respect someone's religious beliefs? Or to have your own beliefs respected? Many believers in God insist that their religion deserves to be respected, even by nonbelievers, but what exactly are they asking for? They may simply be asking to be let alone in their beliefs, which is quite a reasonable request. It is rare that anyone who asks to be let alone is denied this. They may be asking that their right to believe be honored, which is surely fair. Certainly, in the West few Christians have any trouble with their right to believe being infringed upon; however, some people may be seen to be asking for much more.

Writer Austin Cline suggests,

> These people may accuse atheists of intolerance not because atheists are infringing on anyone's right to believe, or because they are going around badgering others, but rather because atheists are expressing criticism of the content of those beliefs. So, it can be argued that what religious believers are *really* asking for is deference, reverence, high regard, admiration, esteem, and other things which their beliefs (or any beliefs, opinions, ideas, etc.) are not automatically entitled to. [1]

Such people English philosopher Simon Blackburn (1944–) describes as demonstrating "respect creep," and he frames the issue rather directly. Few, if any, irreligious atheists have a problem with "respecting" religion if we simply mean letting believers go about their rituals, worship, religious practices, etc., at least so long as those practices don't negatively impact others. At the same time, though, few irreligious atheists will agree to "respect" religion if we mean admiring it, having high regard for it as a superior way to live, or deferring to the demands believers make on behalf of their beliefs and practices. People may start out by insisting on respect in the minimal sense, and in a generally liberal world they may not find it too difficult to obtain it. But then what we might call respect creep sets in, where the request for minimal toleration turns into a demand for more substantial respect, such as fellow-feeling, or esteem, and finally deference and reverence. In the limit, unless you let me take over your mind and your life, you are not showing proper respect for my religious or ideological convictions. Respect is thus a complex concept that involves a spectrum of possible attitudes rather than a simple yes or no. People can and do respect ideas, things, and other people in one or two ways, but not in others. This is normal and expected.

We can respect, in the minimal sense of tolerating, those who hold false beliefs. We can pass by on the other side. We need not be concerned to change them, and in a liberal society we do not seek to suppress them or silence them. But once we are convinced that a belief is false, or even just that it is irrational, we cannot respect in any thicker sense those who hold it—not on account of their holding it. We may respect them for all sorts of other qualities, but not that one. We would prefer them to change their minds. Or, if it is to our advantage that they have false beliefs, as in a game of poker, and we are poised to profit from them, we may be wickedly pleased that they are taken in. But that is not a symptom of special substantial respect, but quite the reverse. It is one up to us, and one down to them.

Respecting religion in the sense of tolerating it is usually a fair request; but such minimal respect isn't what religious believers usually want. After all, there is little danger in America of most religious beliefs not being tolerated on a basic level. Some religious minorities may have legitimate concerns in this regard, but they aren't the ones making the most noise about getting respect. Religious believers also don't appear to be interested in simply being "let alone" to go about their religious business. Instead, they seem to want the rest of us to somehow admit or acknowledge just how important, serious, admirable, valuable, and wonderful their religion is. That's how they regard their religion, after all, and sometimes they seem unable to understand why others don't feel the same way. They are asking for and demanding much more than they are entitled to. No matter how important their religion is to them personally, they cannot expect others to treat it in the same way. Religious believers cannot demand that nonbelievers regard their religion with admiration or treat it as a superior way of living.

There's something about religion, religious beliefs, and theism, in particular, which seems to increase a person's sense of entitlement and the demands they make on behalf of it. People can act brutally in the pursuit of political causes, for example, but they seem to act even more brutally when they believe that they have religious or even divine sanction for that cause. God becomes an "amplifier" for whatever happens to be going on; in this context, even more respect, deference, and reverence is expected for religious beliefs and claims than other sorts of beliefs and claims which a person might have. It's not enough that people in the religious community want something; God also wants it and wants it for them. If others don't "respect" this, then they are attacking not just the religious community, but also God as the moral center of their universe. Here, "respect" can't possibly be thought of in the minimalist sense. It can't simply be "tolerance" and instead must be thought of as deference and reverence. Believers want to be treated as special, but irreligious atheists should treat them like everyone else and, perhaps more importantly, treat their religious claims and opinions like any other claim or opinion.

Here I have selected several of what might be called subjective aspects of respect: compassion, morality, reverence, and trust. These are four words with slightly different meanings, but all relate to respect. Different writers have analyzed their meanings, and here I mention some of those considerations, as I believe they bear directly on the respect issue.

19

COMPASSION

Compassion for others is universally accepted as being a desirable human attribute, and most people would agree that this is so regardless of what those others may believe in a religious sense. I see that stance as underlying respect in an essential way. What does it mean to exercise compassion? To discuss the topic of compassion I reference the book by the well-known historian of religion Karen Armstrong, called *12 Steps to a Compassionate Life.*[1] She proposes the "steps" for readers to think about in assessing their own exercise of compassion for others. Here I will simply summarize Armstrong's recommendations for developing compassion.

In her first step, "Learn about Compassion," Armstrong discusses key aspects of compassion in various cultures: In Judaism, the golden rule was well expressed by Hillel in approximately 200 BC. In Islam, there are the key notions of surrender of ego (*islam*) and peace (*salam*). In Buddhist myths, the ideas of *li* (ritual), *shu* (consideration), and *ren* (softness) play important roles. A second step, which Armstrong labels "Look at Your Own World," means examining our own families and community, our immediate "circles of compassion," and how they work. The third step she calls "Compassion for Yourself," which is the necessary starting point for loving one's neighbor as oneself. Armstrong's fourth step is "Empathy," where one tries to feel for others without necessarily suffering excessive personal pain but nevertheless wanting to avoid "false cheerfulness." She especially notes how difficult it is to extend sympathies to people of different cultures. Armstrong's fifth step is "Mindfulness," or dispassionate reflection, which she thinks of as a form of meditation. Her sixth step is "Action," portrayed as what should be an outcome driven directly by meditation.

Step 7 is "How Little We Know," where Armstrong encourages us to broaden our perspective to make a place for others. Here she holds up the classic notion of Socratic dialogue and the premise that, "The unexamined life is not worth living." Reflection on how little we know led philosopher Karl Popper to assert, "We don't know anything," and Einstein, in contemplating the mystical wonder of the universe, to assert, "In this sense I belong to the ranks of devoutly religious men." Armstrong's step 8, "How Should We Speak to One Another?" contrasts effective dialogue with contests in which participants argue to win, and to bludgeon, humiliate, and overcome those who they see as their opponents. In step 9, "Concern for Everybody," she asks us to consider how we speak about foreigners, whether with bigotry, contempt, and/or "tribal egotism."

Step 10, "Knowledge," is simply a suggestion that we make an effort to expand our understanding of other nations' cultures and religions. In step 11, "Recognition," Armstrong focuses on images and how, for example, the image of a young nude Vietnamese girl running away from American bombing made a huge impression in U.S. media and helped turn the tide of the war in Vietnam. Step 12, "Love Your Enemies," is perhaps the most difficult challenge and might be seen by some as a bridge too far. Armstrong quotes Laoze from 300 BC, who taught that violence always reflects on the perpetrator. She also cites Gandhi as saying, "An eye for an eye makes the whole world blind."[2] We are reminded of other examples of compassion, for instance, Nelson Mandela promoting the Truth and Reconciliation Commission in South Africa, the Dalai Lama refusing recrimination against China after his exile from Tibet, and Jesus actively forgiving his executioners. Compassion is a multifaceted but crucial aspect of respect for others.

20

MORAL VIRTUES

We must confront the questions of (1) whether atheists are inherently immoral, and (2) whether the morality of others is the essential criterion for respecting them. I have difficulty with the notion that someone's belief or disbelief in God has anything to do with morality, except as that belief inherently includes intention of an immoral act, as defined here. As for morality being a key criterion for respectability, it seems that it is—else what can we possibly mean by respectability?

So, what does it mean to be moral? Professor Jonathan Haidt (2012), who calls himself a morality psychologist, has proposed six attributes (he calls them "foundations") of human moral behavior. They are as follows:

1. Care/harm (operating out of kindness and concern, never harming others)
2. Liberty/oppression (enhancing opportunities for others, not constraining them)
3. Fairness/cheating (acting in a way that the community considers to be impartial and honest, not taking advantage of others)
4. Loyalty/betrayal (being faithful to commitments and obligations)
5. Authority/subversion (properly exercising power and control given by others, not subverting same)
6. Sanctity/degradation (upholding sacredness of the dignity and rights of others as human beings, not deprecating them)[1]

Haidt discusses in detail how individual differences with respect to these attributes play out in human interactions of all kinds, including politics.

Consider, more generally, how these properties apply to ordinary daily living with one another.

Care/harm is the measure of caring about another person based on understanding of the other person's plans, objectives, and abilities or constraints on that person in fulfilling those plans. Insofar as possible one should try to defer to the other person's actions. A caring person will cause no physical or emotional harm to another person.

Liberty/oppression has to do with one's flexibility in allowing the other person to behave according to that other person's preferences and, insofar as possible, be resilient when that person acts or makes errors that are inconvenient, offering to help as needed.

Fairness/cheating applies to consistency in one's relationship to the other person and not demanding more effort, knowledge, or skill than can be expected from him or her according to social norms. It means helping the other person understand when one's own request is beyond the other person's understanding or capability. It means not taking actions that are in conflict with the other person's apparent intentions unless their safety is at risk, in the latter case explaining why the deviation from what would normally be desired.

Loyalty/betrayal refers to the sense of devotion and obligation to the other person so as to remember, anticipate, and conform to their wants. Insofar as possible it means anticipating the other person's expressed needs and being ready to perform for the user when called upon.

Authority/subversion speaks to making decisions and actions based on knowledge sufficient for the task of serving the other person or the necessary need, in consideration of the other person's objectives, or otherwise operating on the basis of transparent default objectives.

Sanctity/degradation is the measure of politeness in action and speech communication with the other person. It means communicating at a level requested by the user or implied by user language and style. Such communication should be clean, orderly, and as straightforward as possible.

These terms can be thought of as continuous degrees, with the first term for each pair being a generally desirable property of human behavior and the second term being the opposite or undesirable property. This is the stuff of moral psychology and sociology. One cannot assert that these properties are fully independent of one another, given the associations and the complexities that abound in language.

According to Haidt, morality manifests itself intuitively and is generally acknowledged to be immediate as contrasted to much slower judgments based on deliberative considerations. This is the point emphasized in Nobel laureate Daniel Kahneman's (2011) book *Thinking, Fast and Slow*.[2] "Thinking fast" intuition plays a key role in the *confirmation bias*, so well established in human decision-making.[3] This is the tendency to search for, interpret, favor, and recall information in a way that confirms one's preexisting beliefs or hypotheses.

There is the related question of rationality versus rationalization. Haidt discusses how Plato's brother, Glaucon, argued with Socrates that people adopt characteristics based on fear of getting caught and/or building their reputations rather than true altruism. Haidt shows how the mentality of what he calls a WEIRD demographic (Western, educated, industrialized, rich, and democratic) operates with a very different weighting of the aforementioned morality attributes, as compared to people in non-Western societies where family and tradition are the foundation of values. Haidt also shows how the attribute of care/harm is most sacred to political liberals, while that of liberty/oppression is dominant for political libertarians, and for social conservatives all attributes are more or less evenly weighted. There are large individual differences in what people regard as the bases of morality and hence how they behave with respect to one another.

21

REVERENCE

Reverence is a term usually associated with religion, but it need not be, and I see a strong relation to respect. From a broader perspective, reverence can also apply to atheism. The ideas of Paul Woodruff (1943–) on reverence are worthy of consideration here.[1] Woodruff defines reverence as a well-developed capacity to have certain feelings (like awe, respect, and shame). Reverence, he asserts, begins with a deep understanding of human limitations and a capacity to be in awe of whatever we believe to be outside our control, to keep us from acting like gods. Hubris is the opposite of reverence; however, reverence is not to be confused with respect per se. The atheist or the faithful can have much or too little respect. Reverence is the capacity to have feelings, not a feeling in itself. Awe is the most reverent of feelings, but awe is inarticulate. Woodruff asserts that it is virtually impossible to act alone in the exercise of reverence; it is inherently a social activity.

Woodruff claims (going back to ancient times) that Thucydides didn't fear gods, but he feared human arrogance. Socrates asserted that a large component of wisdom is in knowing our own limitations. It was a prevalent Greek idea that reverence grows from acknowledging human weakness. Plato saw reverence as one of the bulwarks of society and played up the idea of reverence for truth. (Plato may have gone a bit far in a proposed replacing of familial love with community: making all the women wives of all the men.) Protagoras stated that without reverence no group of humans can stand by one another; they will perish. Relative to the ancients, Woodruff claims that we have lost not reverence itself, but the idea of reverence.

In ancient Asia, Confucius promoted the idea of *li*. The word is translated in a number of different ways. Most often, *li* is described using some form of the word "ritual," but it has also been translated as *customs*, *etiquette*, *morals*, and *rules of proper behavior*. Reverence is often reinforced by ceremony. Without reverence, rituals are said to be empty. To Confucius, reverence leads to ceremony and the feelings that make ceremony worthwhile. Unfortunately, we are losing many of the ceremonial occasions in which people find ways to be reverent. *Li* does not stand against change, but regulates and orders it. *Li* does not impose hierarchy, but makes it harmonious. For Confucius, a human being without the feeling of modesty (*ci*) and deference (*rang*) is not human.

Many of our religious leaders are traditionally called "reverend," implying religious status. Yet, Woodruff claims that reverence has more to do with politics and community than religion. He suggests that if you wish to be reverent, never claim that God supports your political views. That claim opts you out of the political process. If a religious group thinks it speaks and acts as God commands, that can justify violence, and this is not reverence. According to Woodruff, God-fearing is not reverence, since awe is not fear. Religion without reverence is common, although a pity; politics without reverence is catastrophic. What we admire in religions that are not our own tradition is not faith (in that other religion), but the reverence of those believers. Yet, because worship is based on faith, faith can be arrogant, therefore not reverent. Faith-centered religion may place a low value on reverence. When rising doubts cloud the certainty of religious claims, reverence is all the more important. Reverence cannot be expressed in a creed. According to Woodruff, its most fundamental expression is said to be music.

Reverence is claimed to defy conversion into rule-based ethics. There are no rules for being courteous or grieving, for example. Patriotism can be a virtue when a country follows justice. Justice demands reverence, otherwise it can tear people apart. Woodruff suggests that if you desire peace in the world, do not pray that everyone share your beliefs. Pray instead that all may be reverent. In fact, reverent people may not know what to believe. Wars can be fought by reverent people. Reverence may be true even though beliefs may be false. Humility is not despair, and it is not skepticism.

Woodruff points out that, in learning communities, good teachers listen to their pupils, and in this they are reverent. When teachers are silent it is the student who must speak. Part of good teaching is the ability to discover good things about people and show awe at subject matter that cannot be tamed. Without reverence an instructor is not a teacher, a boss is not a leader, and a house is not a home. We know reverence firsthand when we are at home, but failures of reverence at home are the most devastating.

22

TRUST

Trust is a topic that has been left outside of science until fairly recently when economists and psychologists picked it up. A new journal called *Trust Research* appeared in 2011.[1] System engineers concerned with safety have become especially interested in trust. Whether this technical research can apply to trust in God is an open question.

To a great extent, respect involves trust, at least a tendency or an effort to trust. There are multiple factors that engender trust between and among people. Most obvious is reliability, whether a person or an institution has consistently performed well or as expected, and did not fail. Immediately following a failure or breach we are inclined not to trust. Distrust can be irrational in the case where an otherwise reliable person commits a rare failure and takes pains to acknowledge the failure and make serious effort to prevent failing in the future. If the failure was in the long past and recent behavior has been acceptable, we are inclined to trust.

We tend to trust people and things that are familiar, events that we think we understand and have experienced. For this reason, we adhere to beliefs and cultural norms held by our parents and friends growing up— in short, our tribe. Unfamiliar people and situations provide insufficient statistical evidence on which to base trust. We also tend to trust people and institutions that we depend on, perhaps because we must (we may have no choice), but also because those entities are familiar. Commercial advertising is a greater determiner of what we trust than we are willing to admit.

Trust may be based on evidence that is not direct but secondhand. Having initial trust in a person or institution, we are inclined to trust something that person or institution says or does. Experiments and models of trust are now becoming more popular in various fields of science and technology, especially psychology (interpersonal trust), computer science (cybersecurity and the operation of such complex systems as air traffic control), and political science.

Trust has been defined as a human's propensity to submit to vulnerability and unpredictability, and nevertheless to continue a relationship. Various authors have opined on the bases for trust, but here I will make use of my own taxonomy for a detailed breakdown.[2] (These were originally developed by the author as bases for trusting technology.) I assert that these may be called *objective* bases, since conceivably they are measurable by objective means and can be distinguished from subjective (affective) attributes like those described earlier as moral virtues. Thus, I would assert that we trust because of the following:

1. Statistical reliability: lack of error or failure of the other person(s) to adhere to expectations or accepted standards
2. Usefulness: ability of the other person(s) to do what is most important, what is most successful or beneficial
3. Flexibility: ability of the other person(s) to adjust to circumstances in fulfilling expectations
4. Understandability: ability of the other person(s) to clarify how and why they are doing what they are doing
5. Explication of intent: ability of the other person(s) to communicate what they will do next
6. Familiarity: assuming the behavior of the other person(s) based on past experience
7. Dependence: the degree to which one has no choice but to depend on the other person(s)

The first five are properties of the other person(s), while the last two are properties of the person doing the trusting.

THE PRISONER'S DILEMMA GAME

The dilemma of when and how much to trust—to submit oneself to unpredictability and vulnerability—is dramatically illustrated in two-party "contest" situations. These are common in interpersonal relations, business situations, and international politics, where each of two parties is trying to maximize their own gain, and where the payoff (gain or loss) for each depends on not only which move a first player makes, but also which move the second player makes.

I have always been fascinated by the social trust implications of the so-called prisoner's dilemma game. This can be modeled as a *formal game*, as illustrated here. There are many kinds of formal games. Games can be two-player or multiplayer. The examples here are only of the two-player type. Consider the two payoff matrices in figure 22.1. The first number in each cell is the corresponding payoff (or penalty) to oneself, and the second number is the payoff (or penalty) to the opponent. The example on the left is a so-called zero-sum game, where one party's gain is the other party's loss.

For any game situation, a most conservative strategy is called a *minimax*, in which one chooses the option with the least downside risk, whatever the opponent does. For example, in the matrix at left in the figure one's own minimax is A, since it is the best of the worst outcomes, no matter what move the opponent makes. (If one's own decision is A, the worst of –3 and –1 is –3. If one's own decision is B, the worst of –4 and –5 is –5, so the best of –3 and –5 is –3, pointing to A as the minimax

OWN DECISION \ OPPONENT DECISION	X	Y
A	-3, 3	-1, 1
B	-4, 4	-5, 5

OWN DECISION \ OPPONENT DECISION	X	Y
A	-2, -2 R, R	-10, -1 S, T
B	-1,-10 T, S	-6, -6 P, P

Figure 22.1. Dominating and nondominating strategies (at left) and prisoner's dilemma (right). ***Author's drawing***

decision.) The opponent's minimax is seen to be X. (This is because the worst of 3 and 4 is 3 for X, and the worst of 1 and 5 is 1 for Y, so the best of these is 3, pointing to X as the minmax.)

A game situation with an interesting history and moral lessons is called *prisoner's dilemma*. An example is shown at the right in figure 22.1. The situation is named for the dilemma a prisoner has in deciding whether to keep silent about his fellow prisoner (cooperate) or provide harmful testimony about him and gain a lighter sentence (defect). In the matrix at right, the upper left cell is mutual cooperation, both keeping quiet about the crime (both "rewarded" [R] with a light sentence). The lower right cell is mutual defection, testifying against the other (both "punished" with P). The other two cells are where one "testifies" (T) against the other and wins a light sentence, while the other tries to cooperate but becomes a "sucker" (S) with a heavy sentence.

Thus, if you defect (choose B) while your colleague tries to cooperate (chooses X), you lose little (−1) and he suffers great loss (−10). If you both cooperate (A, X), you both suffer only a minimal loss (−2), while mutual defection (B, Y) results in moderate punishment P for both (−6). Notice that if both players use the normally conservative minimax strategy, the result is mutual defection. Yet, paradoxically, this conservative minimax result (−6 for both players) is significantly worse than the riskier mutual cooperation result (−2 for both). There are plenty of situations that fit those conditions, and those situations can be stated mathematically.[3]

This paradoxical situation is not unlike many situations in politics, business, and personal life, where each party's effort to get the advantage over another party can result in greater cost to both parties than if they cooperate to mutual advantage. But the temptation to defect (use the conservative minimax strategy) is so rational. There seems to be a great moral lesson in this simple game, which many researchers have studied and writers have commented on. Trust pays off, so long as it is mutual, but it risks being vulnerable to being taken advantage of. The challenge for repeated plays is to build mutual trust, knowing that the other guy can defect and play you for a sucker. Work toward trust and mutual cooperation, but be circumspect.

TRUST AND FAITH

Faith in general is defined as the obligation of loyalty or fidelity to a person, promise, engagement, etc. Religious faith is defined as firm belief in something for which there may be no tangible proof: complete trust, confidence, reliance, or devotion. Accordingly, religious belief is said to be based not on physical evidence, but rather faith. Religious faith presumably emanates from trust we have in believing religious texts, people, or institutions that appear to warrant trust themselves and have actively taught us to trust. And those texts, people, and institutions can be said to have acquired their trust in the same manner and so on back in time.

The gospel of John (20:19–31) tells the story of the doubting Thomas, who was skeptical that Jesus had reappeared after being crucified—unless he could see Jesus' wounded hands. Jesus later admonished John and said, "Blessed are those who have not seen and yet have come to believe." It's in the Bible, and for many the Bible is the accepted basis for faith.

When is faith (or trust) based on nothing more than tradition? Is the only justification for depending on faith a lack of evidence? How much of faith is simply hope regarding preferred outcomes for some future events?

One can certainly contend that science is a matter of faith: faith that use of scientific method based on evidence will allow us to infer that some hypothesis is true. Put more broadly, one must have faith in a value system to underpin any interpretation.

Philosopher Daniel Dennett likens religious faith to falling in love. He claims that the language of romantic love and the language of religious devotion are all but indistinguishable. Neither faith nor romantic love is rational. Neither is a matter of comparing plusses and minuses to determine a best policy. Loving partners (or business partners) develop trust in one another, and defection from that trusting relation can destroy that relationship rather quickly.

23

IGNORANCE AND INNOVATION

Chapter 17 proposes that God be thought of as everything we experience but do not understand. It is suggested that such ignorance be respected and appreciated as a challenge to our tendency to believe we know the truth about the creation of our world and the basis for what we call miracles. One metaphorical thought experiment suggests that you draw a circle around everything that you know (which, of course, is impossible, but let's suppose for a moment that you could). Then everything outside the circle is by definition what you don't know. Clearly, no matter how big the circle, everything outside is infinity. Admission of this ignorance is an antidote to the hubris of complacent theistic belief that, "God did it, that explains it, and end of story."

Stuart Firestein's little book titled *Ignorance* makes the point that it is ignorance, not knowledge, that drives science, and hence innovation and new understanding.[1] Ignorance, duly respected, drives curiosity, and curiosity determines how scientists program their efforts. Firestein likens science to looking for a cat in a dark room, even though there may not be a cat. The point was made earlier that the "scientific method" is an underlying myth that is helpful in explaining what scientists think they are doing, and how they explain it to others, but that in reality science is largely hit or miss. That same attitude of respect for one's ignorance, a curiosity of how best to focus one's efforts, and a willingness to hit sometimes and to miss at other times, can apply to respecting other people, and, in turn, hopefully gaining respect.

Ignorance makes for variety, and variety precipitates learning and improvement. Not knowing how others have solved life's problems requires one to try different approaches, some of which are bound to differ from those used before by others. This makes for a variety in approaches and experiences. This is akin to random genetic mutations, which in Darwinian theory is how the species adapts to new environments and improves its lot. Evolutionists call it "requisite variety," which eventually leads to some failures and some successes, but in the long run the successes prevail. In computer science there are "genetic algorithms" that randomly try different approaches to finding successively better (cheaper, quicker) solutions, where the computer retains the current best one, then keeps trying to improve on that foothold. Respect for the unknown, coupled with effort to discover and make things better, is the key to improving life for everyone. Appreciation of one's own ignorance of others' beliefs can motivate communication and deeper understanding of where the other person is coming from.

24

THE DELICATE TRADE-OFFS IN "LOVING ONE'S NEIGHBOR AS ONESELF"

So, after all this talk about respecting others, what are the reasonable limits of respect? How to "love one's neighbor as oneself," when that neighbor is a lying, hateful, racist, and generally despicable individual? (I won't name examples.)

First, recall that one of Karen Armstrong's principles of compassion is that we must love ourselves. This means being aware of our own feelings as a guide to how we feel about others. She points out that we sometimes attack people for precisely the qualities we dislike in ourselves. Then it seems appropriate that we gently but confidently (two words that are not conflicting) stand up for our own beliefs when necessary, expressing the caveat that we are willing to be convinced otherwise.

But surely our respect for the other's right of belief, and respect for the other's actual behavior and assertions, are different. There are limits, which then poses a trade-off. There must be some balance as when to keep silent and when to speak up, when to humbly accept the other's statements or behavior and when to counter. Rationality might put it in terms of benefit to one's self versus benefit to the other, or to society. There is a hedonism versus altruism issue here that is larger than just scoring debating points. Everyone chooses, consciously or unconsciously, where to draw the line. All that can be hoped for is that each person thinks to some extent about the issue and trades benefits and costs fairly. This applies to differing beliefs about God and expressions of those beliefs. Accepting another person's beliefs about God is very different from accepting that person's beliefs or actions that amount to hatred, prejudice, or mental or bodily harm to others.

Physicist/humanist Alan Lightman makes the following assertion regarding others' right of belief, particularly with regard to statements about our physical world:

> I respect the notions of God and other divine beings; however, I insist on one thing. I insist that any statements made by such beings and their prophets about the material world, including statements recorded in the sacred books, must be subject to the experimental testing of science. In my view, the truths of such statements cannot be assumed. They must be tested and revised or rejected as needed. The spiritual world, and the world of the Absolutes, have their own domain. The physical world should be the province of science.[1]

And in another place, while pondering the dilemma between science and faith, he states,

> I will end this day listening to Bach's exquisite *Mass in B Minor*, written to celebrate a Christian God. I will take it to celebrate all gods, for the gods of our faiths are not so different from each other. I will take it to celebrate those who believe and those who do not, for we all want to believe in something. I will take it to celebrate life in its myriad forms, even as that life passes away. I will take it to celebrate meaning, even if that meaning is only the moment. The moment is now.[2]

CONCLUSION

In this book I review the nature of religious belief, including both ancient and modern arguments for God. I also discuss the nature of science and scientific modeling. Finally, I examine what it means to respect others who have different beliefs and the nature of compassion, reverence, and trust. These are the components that constitute my own outlook on life and particularly justify my calling myself an atheist, a Christian atheist, if you would allow that, since so much of Jesus' teaching still speaks to me.

Atheists throughout history, and especially the "new atheists," have encountered disrespect and even hostility, at least partly for what is sometimes seen as adamant rejection of what others hold dear. As atheism, or just lack of interest in religion, seems to be growing, traditional believers sometimes feel threatened or resentful that others do not respect their beliefs.

History shows that primitive peoples used myths to explain to themselves things that were mysterious. Those myths were their models, their ways of representing truth. Today, such myths do not have the denotative attributes of scientific representations that have emerged since the Enlightenment. Early peoples worshipped the sun, which was somewhat rational since the sun is our known source of energy and sustainer of life. Some would say mankind has regressed to worship of anthropomorphic entities characterized, for example, by divine revelation and virgin birth.

In the secular world, we have a record of accomplishment through use of conscious imagination, scientific experimentation, analysis, and modeling; however, most of current society has not evolved very far from clinging to those old beliefs of an omnipotent, omniscient, supernatural God "up there" who loves us and hears our prayers. There is evidence that for many people, belief in a supernatural God provides happiness and sustains health. Others are content and fare just fine with daily lives in a secular society that respects rationality as a basis for thinking and action. Surely everyone is entitled to his or her own beliefs, whether logical or illogical. Many would say that religion appears to support a double standard when contrasted to daily intellectual pursuits in the otherwise secular world. Yet, we cannot get away from metaphor, myth, and forms of connotative language for the things we hold most dear: our feelings, our passions, our loves.

Modern critical thinkers about cosmology and the origins of life, including theologians, scientists, and other laity, are rapidly abandoning traditional perspectives in favor of a reverent sense of mystery and an appreciation of evolution; however, in a sense we are right back to the attitude of our primitive ancestors. Theologians ask us to believe in a transcendent God as a means to cope with the mystery. But that seems circular, since by definition a transcendent entity is not amenable to expression in tractable human language. Scientists admit that we just don't know how it all began.

One philosophical perspective insists that reality can only be known through models based on denotative (scientific) language and that connotative (metaphorical) language is insufficient. The argument is made that if we can model something denotatively, then we feel that we know that something well enough to communicate it to others unambiguously. Scientific modeling is also important because the effort to model forces us to think hard about what we really believe.

However, most people would agree that there are ways of knowing that are unrelated to what can be dealt with by science. Surely we "know" our own experiences, many of which are personal and cannot be shared. And some experiences are profound, many would say religious, while others would say *transcendent*. One can quibble, as we did earlier in the book, that it is difficult or impossible to say what transcendent means. Nevertheless, we feel it and simply say to others, "You know what I mean."

The contrast in the language and considerations of science with those of religion reveals a stark difference in modes of thinking. This is a difference long recognized but continuing to puzzle and alienate people on both sides of the divide. In any case, it seems that both modes of thinking are essential to our lives.

The mystery aspect of ultimate reality need not be discouraging. As the old saying goes, the more you know, the more you know what you don't know. And that is a nonconverging process. We don't know and don't have a scientific explanation for what seems most important.

We conclude that we cannot apply science to represent the nature of a supernatural God per se, as there is nothing there to model that humans are capable of understanding or talking about. Words like "transcendent" used by theists are not amenable to human understanding, since by their very meaning they refer to what is beyond ordinary human language. I would make the comparison to the concept of *infinity*, which is defined as a mathematical limit, beyond comprehension.

Quite apart from understanding the nature of "God" I agree with those who assert that religious *practice* should not be immune from being tested by efforts at scientific modeling. In contrast, scientific investigations of God per se are doomed to failure for reasons discussed in the book. We can and have modeled human beings in their many kinds of activities, so why not religious practices, which are human activities. Efforts at such modeling should penetrate further into why people believe and what (they say) they believe. This will help us examine ourselves and our culture more thoroughly.

Religious institutions can move toward distinguishing and accepting the disparate but essential roles in life of *logos* and *mythos*, reasoned discourse in denotative modeling, on the one hand, and legitimate subjective feelings expressed through metaphor, on the other. Primitive peoples made little distinction between these ways of thinking. Modern religious institutions often do much the same. It would be desirable to make clear which is being assumed.

It would be healthy to admit that the religious tradition of saying man is made in the image of God is to say nothing sensible, because the old God cannot be modeled and there is no clear and understandable image as to God's constitution or function. Clearly, God is really conceived, at least to a great extent, in the image of man: just the reverse of the traditional phrase.

I argued earlier that "God" could become a useful metaphor for what we don't know and don't understand. God would be conceived not as a supernatural reality to be worshipped, but rather as a truth about our deepest experience and our uncertainty—to be respected, as a truth about ourselves in relation to the universe. Then God could be "believed" in that sense. Such an orientation would discourage hubris and promote reverence and awe for the wonder and beauty of the natural world. It would encourage people to take responsibility for shaping life rather than depending on God to do it.

With this perspective, the new "believer" can still (metaphorically) "know God" in his heart, and "know God" in the beauty of nature, in the faces of children and in the good deeds that people do for other people. Reverence, as described earlier, which has nothing necessarily to do with religion and belief in something supernatural, is highly relevant in this respect.

Intellectual honesty for the respectful atheist means admitting to disbelief in the supernatural while embracing metaphor and recognition of the subjective factors in life that are so difficult (but not necessarily impossible) to fit into a scientific framework.

Clearly, knowing the origin of the universe is beyond the capability of science. The impermanence of everything around us makes us wonder where we can find absolutes that might provide meaning for our existence. We need to rethink our religious institutions to promote secular reverence for those things in life here and now that we find most worthy, wonderful, and beautiful. We need new efforts at community participation to promote caring and faith in one another that can be spread throughout the world. That in no way diminishes the role of metaphor for communicating and engaging participation. Bring on the metaphor, and let God be a metaphor for mystery.

Indeed, we need to redefine God to be all of what we don't understand about our natural surround, a new kind of God that demands our utmost respect for the unknown and our own ignorance and limitations. Others will see it differently. Based on their own particular upbringing and experience they will hold fundamentally different perspectives. That right must be respected. Hopefully, with sufficient modesty in communicating one's beliefs to others, the respectful atheist can gain respect from the believer.

NOTES

PREFACE

1. Thomas Sheridan, *What Is God? Can Religion Be Modeled?* (Washington DC: New Academia Publishing, 2014).

2. Osher Lifelong Learning Institute, Tufts University, Medford, Massachusetts.

INTRODUCTION

1. Anthony DeStefano, *Inside the Atheist Mind* (Nashville, TN: Thomas Nelson, 2018).

2. DeStefano, *Inside the Atheist Mind.*

3. Lee Billings, "Atheism Is Inconsistent with the Scientific Method, Prize-winning Physicist Says," *Scientific American*, March 20, 2019, https://www.scientificamerican.com/article/atheism-is-inconsistent-with-the-scientific-method-prizewinning-physicist-says/ (accessed August 16, 2019).

4. Among the Greek philosophers the term "logos" actually had different meanings. According to Max Weber there is "instrumental rationality" determined by "expectations as to behavior of objects in the environment of other human beings, where these expectations are used as conditions or means for the attainment of the actor's own rationally pursued and calculated ends." Separate is "value rationality," determined by a "conscious belief in the value for its own sake of some ethical, aesthetic, religious, or other form of behavior, independently of its prospects for success."

5. Michael Martin, *Atheism, Morality, and Meaning* (Buffalo, NY: Prometheus, 2002).

6. Martin, *Atheism, Morality, and Meaning.*

1. ORIGINS OF BELIEF

1. "Egyptian Gods and Goddesses," *Ancientegypt.co.uk*, https://www.google.com/search?q=egyptian+gods%2C+ancientegypt.co.uk&rlz=1C5CHFA_enUS802US802&oq=egyptian+gods%2C+ancientegypt.co.uk&aqs=chrome..69i57j33.33559j0j7&sourceid=chrome&ie=UTF-8 (accessed August 18, 2020).

2. "Mythology," *Encyclopedia Mythica*, https://pantheon.org/encyclopedia%20mythca (accessed August 18, 2020).

3. "Greek and Roman Gods," *MIStupid.com*, http://mistupid.com/mythology/index.htm (accessed August 18, 2020).

4. "Greek and Roman Gods."

5. "Greek and Roman Gods."

6. "Greek and Roman Gods."

7. "Greek and Roman Gods."

8. Reza Aslan, *Zealot: The Life and Times of Jesus of Nazareth* (New York: Random House, 2013).

9. Julian Jaynes, *The Origin of Consciousness in the Breakdown of the Bicameral Mind* (Boston: Houghton Mifflin, 1976).

10. Various scholars have documented a change from oral communication, especially including poetry, to communication in written form. Among them is Eric Havelock of Harvard. See his *Preface to Plato* (Cambridge, MA: Harvard University Press, 1963) and *The Muse Learns to Write* (New Haven, CT: Yale University Press, 1986).

11. Jaynes, *The Origin of Consciousness in the Breakdown of the Bicameral Mind*, 436.

12. Leo Sher, "Neuroimaging, Auditory Hallucinations, and the Bicameral Mind," *Journal of Psychiatry and Neurology* 25, no. 3 (May 2000): 239–40.

13. "The Sophists," *Stanford Encyclopedia of Philosophy*, https://plato.stanford.edu/entries/sophists/ (accessed August 18, 2020).

14. "Mark the Evangelist," *Wikipedia*, https://en.wikipedia.org/wiki/Mark_the_Evangelist (accessed August 18, 2020).

15. "Saint Augustine," *Stanford Encyclopedia of Philosophy*, https://plato.stanford.edu/entries/augustine/ (accessed August 18, 2020).

16. "Islam: Empire of Faith: Muhammad," *PBS.org*, www.pbs.org/empires/islam/profilesmuhammed (accessed August 18, 2020).

17. "Shia–Sunni Relations," *Wikipedia*, https://en.wikipedia.org/wiki/ Shia–Sunni (accessed August 18, 2020).

18. "The Crusades," *Global Ministries, United Methodist Church*, http:// gbgm-umc.org/umw/bible/crusades.stm (accessed August 18, 2020).

19. "Isaac Luria," *Wikipedia*, https://en.wikipedia.org/wiki/ Isaac Luria (accessed August 18, 2020).

20. "Martin Luther," *Wikipedia*, https://en.wikipedia.org/wiki/ Martin _ Luther (accessed August 18, 2020).

21. "John Calvin," *Wikipedia*, https://en.wikipedia.org/wiki/ John_Calvin (accessed August 18, 2020).

22. "René Descartes," *Wikipedia*, https://en.wikipedia.org/wiki/ Rene_Descartes (accessed August 18, 2020).

23. "Blaise Pascal," *Wikipedia*, https://en.wikipedia.org/wiki/ Blaise _ Pascal (accessed August 18, 2020).

24. "Isaac Newton," *Wikipedia*, https://en.wikipedia.org/wiki/ Isaac _ Newton (accessed August 18, 2020).

25. "Baruch Spinoza," *Stanford Encyclopedia of Philosophy*, https://plato.stanford.edu/entries/spinoza/ (accessed August 18, 2020).

26. "Spinozism," *Wikipedia*, https://en.wikipedia.org/wiki/Spinozism (accessed August 18, 2020).

27. Matthew R. Cosgrove, "Thomas Aquinas on Anselm's Argument," Commemorative Issue: Thomas Aquinas, 1224–1274, *Review of Metaphysics* 27, no. 3 (March 1974): 513–30.

28. "John Locke," *Stanford Encyclopedia of Philosophy*, https://plato.stanford.edu/entries/locke/ (accessed August 18, 2020).

29. "Henry More," *Stanford Encyclopedia of Philosophy*, https://plato.stanford.edu/entries/henry-more/ (accessed August 18, 2020).

30. "David Hume," *Stanford Encyclopedia of Philosophy*, https://plato.stanford.edu/entries/hume/ (accessed August 18, 2020).

31. Immanuel Kant, *Critique of Pure Reason* (Charleston, SC: Nabu/Amazon Press, 2012). Originally published in 1781.

32. "Denis Diderot," *Internet Encyclopedia of Philosophy*, https:// iep.utm.edu/diderot/ (accessed August 18, 2020).

33. "Ludwig Feuerbach," *Stanford Encyclopedia of Philosophy*, https://plato.stanford.edu/entries/ludwig-feuerbach/ (accessed August 18, 2020).

34. "Friedrich Nietzsche," *Stanford Encyclopedia of Philosophy*, https://plato.stanford.edu/entries/nietzsche/ (accessed August 18, 2020).

2. TRADITIONAL "PROOFS" OF GOD

1. "Saint Anselm," *Stanford Encyclopedia of Philosophy*, https://plato.stanford.edu/entries/anselm/ (accessed August 18, 2020).

2. "Cosmological Argument," *Wikipedia*, https://enwikipedia.org/wiki/Cosmological argument (accessed August 18, 2020).

3. "Samuel Clarke," *Wikipedia*, https://enwikipedia.org/wiki/ Samuel Clarke (accessed August 18, 2020).

4. "Watchmaker Analogy," *Wikipedia*, https://enwikipedia.org/wiki/Watchmaker_analogy (accessed August 18, 2020).

5. Sam Harris, *The Moral Landscape: How Science Can Determine Human Values* (New York: Free Press, 2010).

6. "Blaise Pascal," *Stanford Encyclopedia of Philosophy*, https://plato.stanford.edu/entries/pascal/ (accessed August 18, 2020).

7. "Russell's Teapot," *Wikipedia*, https://enwikipedia.org/wiki/ Russell's teapot (accessed August 18, 2020).

8. "Ludwig Wittgenstein," *Internet Encyclopedia of Philosophy*, https://iep.utm.edu/wittgens/ (accessed August 18, 2020).

3. MORE RECENT THEISTIC ARGUMENTS

1. William Craig and Q. Smith, *Theism, Atheism, and Big Bang Cosmology* (Oxford, UK: Clarendon, 1993), n.p.

2. Victor Stenger, *God: The Failed Hypothesis* (Amherst, NY: Prometheus, 2007).

3. Alvin Plantinga, *Where the Conflict Really Lies* (New York: Oxford University Press, 2012).

4. Richard Swinburne, *Epistemic Justification* (Oxford, UK: Clarendon, 2001). See also Richard Swinburne, *The Existence of God*, 2nd ed. (Oxford, UK: Clarendon, 2010).

5. "Ockham's Razor," *Wikipedia*, https://enwikipedia.org/wiki/ Occam's _ razor (accessed August 18, 2020).

6. "Robert McKenzie Beverley," *Wikipedia*, https://enwikipedia.org/wiki/ Robert_McKenzie_Beverley (accessed August 18, 2020).

7. Pierre Lecomte du Noüy, *Human Destiny* (New York: Arden Library, 1981).

8. William James, *The Varieties of Religious Experience: A Study on Human Nature* (CreateSpace, 2009). Originally published in 1902.

9. "The Varieties of Religious Experience," *Wikipedia*, https:// en.wikipedia.org/wiki/The_Varieties_of_Religious_Experience (accessed August 18, 2020).

10. "The Varieties of Religious Experience."

11. "The Varieties of Religious Experience."

12. "The Varieties of Religious Experience."

13. "The Varieties of Religious Experience."

14. "The Varieties of Religious Experience."

15. "Paul Tillich," *Wikipedia*, https://en.wikipedia.org/wiki/Paul_Tillich (accessed August 18, 2020).

16. Martin Rees, *Just Six Numbers: The Deep Forces That Shape the Universe* (New York: Basic Books, 2000).

4. ACQUIRING KNOWLEDGE

1. Richard Dawkins, *The God Delusion* (Boston: Houghton Mifflin, 2006).

2. Thomas Sheridan, *Modeling Human-System Interaction* (New York: Wiley, 2017).

3. Noam Chomsky, *Syntactic Structures* (Cambridge, MA: MIT Press, 1957).

4. B. F. Skinner, *The Behavior of Organisms: An Experimental Analysis* (Englewood Cliffs, NJ: Prentice-Hall, 1938).

5. "Francis Bacon," *Stanford Encyclopedia of Philosophy*, https://plato.stanford.edu/entries/francis-bacon/ (accessed August 18, 2020).

6. "Karl Popper," *Stanford Encyclopedia of Philosophy*, https://plato.stanford.edu/entries/popper/ (accessed August 18, 2020).

7. Mark S. Frankel, "The Role of Science in Making Good Decisions," *American Association for the Advancement of Science*, June 10, 1998, https:// www.aaas.org/resources/role-science-making-good-decisions (accessed August 18, 2020).

8. Thomas Kuhn, *The Structure of Scientific Revolutions*, 2nd ed. (Chicago: University of Chicago Press, 1970).

9. "Logical Reasoning," *Fibonicci.com*, https://www.fibonicci.com/logical-reasoning/ (accessed August 18, 2020).

10. Donald A. Cress, *René Descartes: Meditations on First Philosophy* (Indianapolis, IN: Hackett, 1979).

11. "Charles Sanders Peirce," *Wikipedia*, https://en.wikipedia.org/wiki/Charles_Sanders_Peirce (accessed August 18, 2020).

12. W. Ross Ashby, *An Introduction to Cybernetics* (New York: John Wiley and Sons, 1956).

13. "Edwin Hubble," *Wikipedia*, https://en.wikipedia.org/wiki/Edwin_Hubble (accessed August 18, 2020).

14. "Aristotle," *Stanford Encyclopedia of Philosophy*, https://plato.stanford.edu/entries/aristotle/ (accessed August 18, 2020).

15. "Saint Anselm," *Stanford Encyclopedia of Philosophy*, https://plato.stanford.edu/entries/anselm/ (accessed August 18, 2020).

16. Raymond S. Nickerson, "Confirmation Bias: A Ubiquitous Phenomenon in Many Guises," *Review of General Psychology* 2, no. 2 (1998): 175. See also Daniel Kahneman, *Thinking, Fast and Slow* (New York: Farrar, Straus and Giroux, 2014).

17. Joseph Campbell, *The Hero with a Thousand Faces* (Novato, CA: New World Library, 1949).

5. MODELING, A CRITERION OF KNOWING

1. Stephen Hawking, *The Theory of Everything* (Mumbai, India: Jaico Publishing House, 2006).

2. S. S. Stevens, *Handbook of Experimental Psychology* (New York: Wiley, 1951).

3. Ockham's razor is attributed to his discussion in Book II of Ockham's *Commentary on the Sentences of Peter Lombard*, the latter being a biblical commentary (1495).

4. Thomas Sheridan, *Modeling Human-System Interaction* (New York: Wiley, 2017).

5. Sheridan, *Modeling Human-System Interaction*.

6. CAN GOD OR RELIGION BE MODELED?

1. "Meister Eckhart ," *Wikipedia*, https://en.wikipedia.org/wiki/ Meister _ Eckhart (accessed August 18, 2020).

2. Daniel Dennett, *Breaking the Spell* (New York: Penguin, 2006).

7. VARIETY OF BELIEF PERSPECTIVES

1. Emily Dickinson, "Tell All the Truth but Tell It Slant," *Poetry Foundation*, https://www.poetryfoundation.org/poems/56824/tell-all-the-truth-but-tell-it-slant-1263 (accessed August 19, 2020).

2. Gian-Carlo Colombo, "An Analysis of Belief," *Downside Review* 77, no. 247 (Winter 1958): 18–37.

3. David Hume, *Treatise on Human Nature* (London: John Noon, 1739), n.p.

4. Charles Sanders Peirce, *Collected Papers of Charles Sanders Peirce*, ed. Arthur W. Burks (Cambridge, MA: Harvard University Press, 1958).

5. "G. E. Moore," *Wikipedia*, https://en.wikipedia.org/wiki/G._E._Moore (accessed August 18, 2020).

6. Thomas Sheridan, *Modeling Human-System Interaction* (New York: Wiley, 2017).

7. G. Shafer, *A Mathematical Theory of Evidence* (Princeton, NJ: Princeton University Press, 1976).

8. Michael Shermer, *The Believing Brain* (New York: Henry Holt, 2011), 177.

8. DEMOGRAPHICS AND TRENDS

1. Frank Newport, "Most Americans Still Believe in God," *Gallup*, June 29, 2016, https://news.gallup.com/poll/193271/americans-believe-god.aspx (accessed August 19, 2020).

2. "Religion," *Gallup*, https://news.gallup.com/poll/1690/religion.aspx (accessed August 19, 2020).

3. David Crary, "Church Membership in U.S. Plummets Over Past 20 years, Poll Says," *Boston Globe*, April 18, 2019, https://www.bostonglobe.com/news/nation/2019/04/18/church-membership-plummets-over-past-years-poll-says/YBlsnmcoZDJiY8qipWLr5M/story.html (accessed August 19, 2020).

4. Zach Hrynowski, "How Many Americans Believe in God?" *Gallup*, November 8, 2019, https://news.gallup.com/poll/268205/americans-believe-god.aspx (accessed August 19, 2020).

5. "Believer Nation," *Cornell University*, https://ropercenter.cornell.edu/sites/default/files/2018-07/113024.pdf (accessed August 19, 2020).

6. Jeffrey M. Jones, "U.S. Church Membership Down Sharply in Past Two Decades," *Gallup*, April 18, 2019, https://news.gallup.com/poll/248837/church-membership-down-sharply-past-two-decades.aspx (accessed August 19, 2020).

7. "Many Americans Say Other Faiths Can Lead to Eternal Life," *Pew Research Center*, December 18, 2008, https://www.pewforum.org/2008/12/18/many-americans-say-other-faiths-can-lead-to-eternal-life/ (accessed August 19, 2020).

8. Dan Merica, "Pew Survey: Doubt of God Growing Quickly among Millennials," *CNN.com*, June 12, 2012, https://religion.blogs.cnn.com/2012/06/12/

pew-survey-doubt-of-god-growing-quickly-among-millennials/ (accessed August 19, 2020).

9. "Global Christianity: A Report on the Size and Distribution of the World's Christian Population," *Pew Research Center*, December 19, 2011, https://www.pewforum.org/2011/12/19/global-christianity-exec/ (accessed August 19, 2020).

10. "Religion in Europe," *Wikipedia*, https://en.wikipedia.org/wiki/Religion_in_Europe (accessed August 19, 2020).

11. "Three in Five Believe in God" *Ipsos MORI*, September 8, 2003, https://www.ipsos.com/ipsos-mori/en-uk/three-five-believe-god (accessed August 19, 2020).

9. IS CREATIONISM DEAD?

1. National Academy of Sciences, *Science and Creationism: A View from the National Academy of Sciences* (Washington, DC: National Academies Press, 1999).

2. National Academy of Sciences, *Science, Evolution, and Creationism* (Washington, DC: National Academies Press, 2008).

10. THE NEW ATHEISM

1. Christopher Hitchens, *God Is Not Great* (New York: Hachette, 2007).

2. Paul Kurtz, *Science and Religion* (Amherst, NY: Prometheus, 2003).

3. John Gray, *Seven Types of Atheism* (New York: Farrar, Straus and Giroux, 2018).

4. William Empson, *Seven Types of Ambiguity* (London: Hogarth, 1984).

5. Gray, *Seven Types of Atheism*, 6–7.

6. Charles Darwin, *The Origin of Species* (London: John Murray, 1859).

7. "Alfred Russel Wallace," *Wikipedia*, https://en.wikipedia.org/wiki/Alfred_Russel_Wallace (accessed August 19, 2020).

8. Richard Dawkins, *The Blind Watchmaker: Why the Evidence of Evolution Reveals a Universe without Design* (New York: W. W. Norton, 1941).

9. Richard Dawkins, *The God Delusion* (Boston: Houghton Mifflin, 2006).

10. Alvin Plantinga, *Where the Conflict Really Lies* (New York: Oxford University Press, 2012).

11. Francis Collins, *The Language of God* (New York: Free Press, 2006).

12. Michael Martin, *Atheism, Morality, and Meaning* (Amherst, NY: Prometheus, 2002).

13. Sam Harris, *The End of Faith* (New York: W. W. Norton, 2004); Sam Harris, *Letter to a Christian Nation* (New York: Knopf, 2006); Sam Harris, *The Moral Landscape: How Science Can Determine Human Values* (New York: Free Press, 2010).

14. National Academy of Sciences, *Science and Creationism: A View from the National Academy of Sciences* (Washington, DC: National Academies Press, 1999).

15. National Academy of Sciences, *Science, Evolution, and Creationism* (Washington, DC: National Academies Press, 2008).

16. National Academy of Sciences, *Science, Evolution, and Creationism*, n.p.

17. Daniel Dennett, *Breaking the Spell* (New York: Penguin, 2006).

18. Richard Dawkins, *The Selfish Gene* (New York: Oxford University Press, 1976).

19. Leon Wieseltier, "The God Genome," *New York Times*, February 19, 2006, nytimes.com/2006/02/19/books/review/ Wieseltier (accessed August 19, 2020).

20. Edward O. Wilson, *Consilience* (New York: Knopf, 1998).

21. Dean Hamer, *The God Gene: How Faith Is Hardwired into Our Genes* (New York: Doubleday, 2004).

22. "John Polkinghorne," *Gifford Lectures*, https://www.giffordlectures.org/lecturers/john-polkinghorne (accessed August 19, 2020).

23. "God Gene," *Wikipedia*, https://en.wikipedia.org/wiki/God_gene (accessed August 19, 2020).

24. Victor Stenger, *God: The Failed Hypothesis* (Amherst, NY: Prometheus, 2007).

25. Victor Stenger, *The New Atheism* (Amherst, NY: Prometheus, 2009).

11. THE BIG BANG, THE MULTIVERSE, AND A NEW DISCONTINUITY IN OUR PERCEIVED IMPORTANCE

1. "Edwin Hubble," *Wikipedia*, https://en.wikipedia.org/wiki/ Edwin _ Hubble (accessed August 19, 2020).

2. "What Does It Mean When They Say the Universe Is Expanding?" *Library of Congress*, https://www.loc.gov/everyday-mysteries/item/what-does-it-mean-when-they-say-the-universe-is-expanding/ (accessed August 19, 2020).

3. Paul Sutter, "Where's the Edge of the Universe?" *Science and Astronomy* May 27, 2016, https://www.space.com/33005-where-is-the-universes-edge-op-ed.html (accessed August 19, 2020).

4. Alan Lightman, *Searching for Stars on an Island in Maine* (New York: Pantheon, 2018).

5. Lightman, *Searching for Stars on an Island in Maine.*

6. Alejandro Jenkins and Gilad Perez, "Looking for Life in the Multiverse," *Scientific American*, https://www.scientificamerican.com/article/looking-for-life-in-the-multiverse/ (accessed August 19, 2020).

7. Bruce Mazlish, *The Fourth Discontinuity* (New Haven, CT: Yale University Press, 1967).

8. "Nonoverlapping Magisteria," *Wikipedia*, https://en.wikipedia.org/wiki/Non-overlapping_magisteria (accessed August 19, 2020).

12. APPREHENDING REALITY

1. T. B. Sheridan and D. Zeltzer, "Virtual Reality—Really?" in P. E. Agre and D. Schuler, eds., *Reinventing Technology, Rediscovering Community: Critical Explorations of Computing as a Social Practice*, 85–96 (Greenwich, CT: Ablex, 1997).

2. Thomas Sheridan, *Telerobotics, Automation, and Human Supervisory Control* (Cambridge, MA: MIT Press, 1992).

3. This topic is discussed extensively in the MIT Press journal *Presence: Teleoperators and Virtual Environments*. The author and a colleague encountered an interesting situation when the archdiocese of Boston complained that the proposed title of a scientific journal we were launching, *Presence*, was too close to their own publication. We had to add a colon and the words "Teleoperators and Virtual Environments" to satisfy the church, as well as copyright rules.

4. "René Descartes," *Stanford Encyclopedia of Philosophy*, https://plato.stanford.edu/entries/descartes/ (accessed August 18, 2020).

5. P. Zahorik and R. L. Jenison, "Presence as Being-in-the-World," *Presence: Teleoperators and Virtual Environments* 7 (1998): 78–89.

6. J. J. Gibson, *The Ecological Approach to Visual Perception* (Boston: Houghton Mifflin, 1979).

13. METAPHOR, MYTH, AND RELIGIOUS LANGUAGE

1. Janet M. Soskice, *Metaphor and Religious Language* (Oxford, UK: Oxford University Press, 2002), n.p.

2. Robert Ellwood, *The Politics of Myth: A Study of C. G. Jung, Mircea Eliade, and Joseph Campbell* (Albany, NY: State University of New York Press, 1999), n.p.

3. "Paul Tillich," *Wikipedia*, https://en.wikipedia.org/wiki/Paul_Tillich (accessed August 18, 2020).

4. Neil Gilman, *Sacred Fragments: Recovering Theology for the Modern Jew* (Philadelphia, PA: Jewish Publishing Society, 1990).

5. Gilman, *Sacred Fragments*.

6. Gilman, *Sacred Fragments*.

7. Gilman, *Sacred Fragments*.

8. Gilman, *Sacred Fragments*.

9. Gilman, *Sacred Fragments*.

10. Sam Harris, *Letter to a Christian Nation* (New York: Knopf, 2006), 8.

11. Ian Gurvitz, *Deconstructing God* (Self-published, 2011).

14. SPIRITUALITY

1. William James, *Pragmatism* (Amherst, NY: Prometheus, 1991).

2. Dalai Lama, *Ethics for the New Millennium* (New York: Riverhead Books, 1999).

3. Alan Lightman, *The Accidental Universe* (New York: Vintage, 2013). See also *Searching for Stars on an Island in Maine* (New York: Pantheon, 2018).

4. Lightman, *The Accidental Universe*, 52–53.

15. OPPOSING PERSPECTIVES THAT SEEM TO CONVERGE

1. "Man vs. God," *Wall Street Journal*, September 9, 2009, https://www.wsj.com/articles/SB10001424052970203440104574405030643556324 (accessed August 19, 2020).

2. "Man vs. God."

3. "Alfred J. Ayer," *Wikipedia*, https://en.wikipedia.org/wiki/A. J . Ayer (accessed August 19, 2020).

4. "The Non-Realism of Don Cupitt," *Doncupitt.com*, www. doncupitt .com/ non - realism (accessed August 19, 2020).

16. QUESTIONS ABOUT CHURCHGOERS

1. Yann Martel, *Life of Pi* (New York: Harcourt Brace Jovanovich, 2001), 72.

2. Francis Galton and C. S. Lewis, "Statistical Inquiries into the Efficacy of Prayer," *Fortnightly Review* 12, no. 68 (1872): 125–35.

3. Galton and Lewis, "Statistical Inquiries into the Efficacy of Prayer," n.p.

4. "Have Studies Proven That Prayer Can Help Heal the Sick?" *www.StraightDope.com*, November 2, 2000, https://www.straightdope.com/ 21342993/have-studies-proven-that-prayer-can-help-heal-the-sick (accessed August 19, 2020).

5. Meredith Melnick, "Study: Religious Folks Have a Sunnier Outlook," *Time*, November 11, 2011, https://healthland.time.com/2011/11/11/study-relig-ious-folks-have-a-sunnier-outlook/ (accessed August 19, 2020).

6. Lawrence Stark, interview with author, 2000.

7. Daniel Dennett, *Breaking the Spell* (New York: Penguin, 2006).

8. "Religion of Humanity," *Wikipedia*, https://en.wikipedia.org/wiki/Relig-ion_of_Humanity#:~:text=Religion%20of%20Humanity%20(from%20French, Humanity%20in%20France%20and%20Brazil (accessed August 19, 2020).

9. "Humanist Manifesto," *Wikipedia*, https://en.wikipedia.org/wiki/Human-ist_Manifesto (accessed August 19, 2020).

17. REDEFINING GOD,
GOD BY OTHER NAMES

1. Don Cupitt is an English philosopher of religion and scholar of Christian theology. He has been an Anglican priest and a professor at the University of Cambridge, although he is better known as a popular writer, broadcaster, and commentator. "Don Cupitt," *Wikipedia*, https://en.wikipedia.org/wiki/ Don_Cupitt (accessed August 19, 2020).

2. Mitchell Silver, *A Plausible God: Secular Reflections on Liberal Jewish Theology* (New York: Fordham University Press, 2006).

3. Silver, *A Plausible God*, 40.

4. Silver, *A Plausible God*, 40.

18. RESPECTING OTHERS' BELIEFS VERSUS RESPECTING OTHERS' HUMANITY

1. Austin Cline, "Do Religious Believers Deserve Respect?" *LearnReligions.com*, August 28, 2018, https://www.learnreligions.com/should-we-respect-religion-248162 (accessed August 19, 2020).

19. COMPASSION

1. Karen Armstrong, *12 Steps to a Compassionate Life* (New York: Random House, 2011).

2. Armstrong, *12 Steps to a Compassionate Life*, 180.

20. MORAL VIRTUES

1. Jonathan Haidt, *The Righteous Mind* (New York: Random House, 2012).

2. Daniel Kahneman, *Thinking, Fast and Slow* (New York: Farrar, Straus and Giroux, 2014).

3. Raymond S. Nickerson, "Confirmation Bias: A Ubiquitous Phenomenon in Many Guises," *Review of General Psychology* 2, no. 2 (1998): 175–220.

21. REVERENCE

1. Paul Woodruff, *Reverence: Renewing a Forgotten Virtue* (New York: Oxford University Press, 2002).

22. TRUST

1. *Journal of Trust Research* (New York: Routledge/Taylor and Francis).

2. Thomas Sheridan, "Individual Differences in Attributes of Trust in Automation: Measurement and Application to System Design," *Frontiers in Psychology* (2019), https://doi.org/10.3389/fpsyg.2019.01117. See also Thomas Sheridan, "Trustworthiness of Command and Control Systems," in *Proceedings of the IFAC/IFIP/IEA/IFORS Conference on Man-Machine Systems*, 427–31 (Elmsford, NY: Pergamon, 1988).

3. A prisoner's dilemma situation is defined by the constraints $T > R > P > S$ and $R > 0.5 \, (S+T)$.

23. IGNORANCE AND INNOVATION

1. Stuart Firestein, *Ignorance: How It Drives Science* (New York: Oxford University Press, 2012).

24. THE DELICATE TRADE-OFFS IN "LOVING ONE'S NEIGHBOR AS ONESELF"

1. Alan Lightman, *Searching for Stars on an Island in Maine* (New York: Pantheon, 2018), 82.
2. Lightman, *Searching for Stars on an Island in Maine*, 207.

BIBLIOGRAPHY

Angeles, Peter. *Critiques of God*. Amherst, NY: Prometheus, 1997.

Armstrong, Karen. *12 Steps to a Compassionate Life*. New York: Random House, 2011.

———. *The Battle for God*. New York: Ballantine, 2000.

———. *The Case for God*. New York: Knopf, 2009.

———. *The Great Transformation*. New York: Knopf, 2006.

———. *A History of God*. New York: Random House, 1993.

Aslan, Reza. *Zealot: The Life and Times of Jesus of Nazareth* . New York: Random House, 2013.

Barth, Karl. *God Here and Now*. London: Routledge, 1964.

Bering, Jesse. *The Belief Instinct*. New York: W. W. Norton, 2011.

Bilington, Ray. *Religion without God*. Oxford, UK: Routledge, 2002.

Cahn, Steven, and David Shatz. *Questions about God*. New York: Oxford University Press, 2002.

Campbell, Joseph. *Creative Mythology*. New York: Penguin, 1968.

———. *The Hero with a Thousand Faces*. Novato, CA: New World Library, 1949.

———. *The Inner Reaches of Outer Space*. Novato, CA: New World Library, 2001.

———. *The Power of Myth*. New York: Random House, 1991.

———. *Thou Art That*. Novato, CA: New World Library, 2001.

Chomsky, Noam. *Syntactic Structures*. Cambridge, MA: MIT Press, 1957.

Collins, Francis. *The Language of God*. New York: Free Press, 2006.

Colombo, Gian-Carlo. "An Analysis of Belief." *Downside Review* 77, no. 247 (Winter 1958): 18–37.

Comte-Sponville, Andre. *The Little Book of Atheist Spirituality*. New York: Viking, 2006.

Cosgrove, Matthew R. "Thomas Aquinas on Anselm's Argument." Commemorative Issue: Thomas Aquinas, 1224–1274, *Review of Metaphysics* 27, no. 3 (March 1974): 513–30.

Cox, Harvey. *The Future of Faith*. New York: HarperCollins, 2009.

———. *When Jesus Came to Harvard*. New York: Houghton Mifflin, 2004.

Craig, William, and Chad Meister. *God Is Great, God Is Good*. Downers Grove, IL: Intervarsity Press, 2009.

———, and Q. Smith. *Theism, Atheism, and Big Bang Cosmology*. Oxford, UK: Clarendon, 1993.

Cress, Donald A. *René Descartes: Meditations on First Philosophy*. Indianapolis, IN: Hackett, 1979.

Cunningham, George. *Decoding the Language of God*. New York: Prometheus, 2010.

Dalai Lama. *Ethics for the New Millennium*. New York: Riverhead Books, 1999.

Darwin, Charles. *The Origin of Species*. London: John Murray, 1859.

Dawkins, Richard. *The Blind Watchmaker: Why the Evidence of Evolution Reveals a Universe without Design*. New York: W. W. Norton, 1941.
———. *The God Delusion*. Boston: Houghton Mifflin, 2006.
———. *The Selfish Gene*. New York: Oxford University Press, 1976.
Dembski, William (ed.). *Mere Creation*. Downers Grove, IL: Intervarsity Press, 1998.
Dennett, Daniel. *Breaking the Spell*. New York: Penguin, 2006.
DeStefano, Anthony. *Inside the Atheist Mind*. Nashville, TN: Nelson Books, 2018.
du Noüy, Pierre Lecomte. *Human Destiny*. New York: Arden Library, 1981.
Ellwood, Robert. *The Politics of Myth: A Study of C. G. Jung, Mircea Eliade, and Joseph Campbell*. Albany, NY: State University of New York Press, 1999.
Empson, William. *Seven Types of Ambiguity*. London: Hogarth, 1984.
Firestein, Stuart. *Ignorance: How It Drives Science*. New York: Oxford University Press, 2012.
Flew, Anthony. *There Is a God*. New York: HarperCollins, 2007.
Franklin, Ralph W. (ed.). *The Poems of Emily Dickinson*. Cambridge, MA: Harvard University Press, 1998.
Fromm, Erich. *Escape from Freedom*. New York: Holt, 1941.
———. *Man for Himself*. New York: Holt, 1990.
Galton, Francis, and C. S. Lewis. "Statistical Inquiries into the Efficacy of Prayer." *Fortnightly Review* 12, no. 68 (1872): 125–35.
Gibson, Arthur. *God and the Universe*. New York: Routledge, 2000.
Gibson, J. J. *The Ecological Approach to Visual Perception*. Boston: Houghton Mifflin, 1979.
Gilman, Neil. *Sacred Fragments: Recovering Theology for the Modern Jew*. Philadelphia, PA: Jewish Publishing Society, 1990.
Gould, Steven Jay. *The Mismeasure of Man*. New York: W. W. Norton, 1981.
Gray, John. *Seven Types of Atheism*. New York: Farrar, Straus and Giroux, 2018.
Greenblatt, Stephen. *The Swerve*. New York: W. W. Norton, 2011.
Greene, Brian. *Fabric of the Cosmos*. New York: Knopf, 2004.
Greene, Garrett. *Imagining God*. San Francisco, CA: Harper and Row, 1989.
Gurvitz, Ian. *Deconstructing God*. Self-published, 2011.
Hagerty, Barbara. *Fingerprints of God*. New York: Penguin, 2009.
Haidt, Jonathan. *The Righteous Mind*. New York: Random House, 2012.
Hamer, Dean. *The God Gene : How Faith Is Hardwired into Our Genes*. New York: Random House, 2005.
Harris, Sam. *The End of Faith*. New York: W. W. Norton, 2004.
———. *Free Will*. New York: Simon and Schuster, 2012.
———. *Letter to a Christian Nation*. New York: Knopf, 2006.
———. *The Moral Landscape: How Science Can Determine Human Values*. New York: Free Press, 2010.
Hart, George. *A Dictionary of Egyptian Gods and Goddesses*. London: Routledge, 1986.
Hawking, Stephen. *The Theory of Everything*. Mumbai, India: Jaico Publishing House, 2006.
Hawkins, Stephen, and L. Mlodinow. *The Grand Design*. New York: Random House, 2010.
Hedges, Chris. *I Don't Believe in Atheists*. New York: Free Press, 2008.
Hitchens, Christopher. *God Is Not Great*. New York: Hachette, 2007.
———. *The Portable Atheist*. Cambridge, MA: DaCapo, 2007.
James, William. *Pragmatism*. Amherst, NY: Prometheus, 1991.
Jaynes, Julian. *The Origin of Consciousness in the Breakdown of the Bicameral Mind*. Boston: Houghton Mifflin, 1976.
Kahneman, Daniel. *Thinking, Fast and Slow*. New York: Farrar, Straus and Giroux, 2014.
Kant, Immanuel. *Critique of Pure Reason*. Charleston, SC: Nabu/Amazon Press, 2012. Originally published in 1781.
Kardong, Kenneth. *Beyond God*. Amherst, NY: Humanity Books, 2010.
Kuhn, Thomas. *The Structure of Scientific Revolutions*, 2nd ed. Chicago: University of Chicago Press, 1970.
Kurtz, Paul. *Science and Religion*. Amherst, NY: Prometheus, 2003.
Lewis, C. S. *The Efficacy of Prayer*. Cincinnati, OH: Forward Movement Publications, 1958.
Lewis, Clive S. *The Question of God*. New York: Free Press, 2002.

Lightman, Alan. *The Accidental Universe.* New York: Vintage, 2013.
―――. *Searching for Stars on an Island in Maine.* New York: Pantheon, 2018.
Luhrmann, T. M. *When God Talks Back.* New York: Random House, 2012.
Martel, Yann. *Life of Pi.* New York: Harcourt Brace Jovanovich, 2001.
Martin, Michael. *Cambridge Companion to Atheism.* New York: Cambridge University Press, 2007.
―――. *Atheism, Morality, and Meaning.* Amherst, NY: Prometheus, 2002.
Mazlish, Bruce. *The Fourth Discontinuity.* New Haven, CT: Yale University Press, 1967.
Miller, James B. (ed.). *Cosmic Questions,* vol. 950. New York: New York Academy of Sciences, 2001.
Nickerson, Raymond S. "Confirmation Bias: A Ubiquitous Phenomenon in Many Guises." *Review of General Psychology* 2, no. 2 (1998): 175–220.
Peirce, Charles Sanders. *Collected Papers of Charles Sanders Peirce.* Ed. Arthur W. Burks. Cambridge, MA: Harvard University Press, 1958.
Plantinga, Alvin. *Where the Conflict Really Lies.* New York: Oxford University Press, 2012.
Popper, Karl. *The Logic of Scientific Discovery.* London: Routledge, 1934.
Preus, J. Samuel. *Explaining Religion.* New Haven, CT: Yale University Press, 1987.
Proctor, Robert, and E. J. Capaldi (eds.). *Psychology of Science: Implicit and Explicit Processes.* New York: Oxford University Press, 2012.
Raymo, Chet. *Skeptics and True Believers.* New York: Walker, 1998.
Rees, Martin. *Just Six Numbers: The Deep Forces That Shape the Universe.* New York: Basic Books, 2000.
Robinson, John A. T. *Honest to God.* Louisville, KY: Westminster John Knox Press, 2002.
Russell, Bertrand. *Why I Am Not a Christian.* New York: Simon and Schuster, 1957.
Shafer, G. *A Mathematical Theory of Evidence.* Princeton, NJ: Princeton University Press, 1976.
Sher, Leo. "Neuroimaging, Auditory Hallucinations, and the Bicameral Mind." *Journal of Psychiatry and Neurology* 25, no. 3 (May 2000): 239–40.
Sheridan, T. B., and D. Zeltzer. "Virtual Reality—Really?" In P. E. Agre and D. Schuler, eds., *Reinventing Technology, Rediscovering Community: Critical Explorations of Computing as a Social Practice,* 85–96. Greenwich, CT: Ablex, 1997.
Sheridan, Thomas. "Individual Differences in Attributes of Trust in Automation: Measurement and Application to System Design." *Frontiers in Psychology* (2019), https://doi.org/10.3389/fpsyg.2019.01117.
―――. *Modeling Human-System Interaction.* New York: Wiley, 2017.
―――. "Trustworthiness of Command and Control Systems." In *Proceedings of the IFAC/IFIP/IEA/IFORS Conference on Man-Machine Systems,* 427–31. Elmsford, NY: Pergamon, 1988.
―――. *What Is God? Can Religion Be Modeled?* Washington, DC: New Academia Publishing, 2014.
Shermer, Michael. *The Believing Brain.* New York: Henry Holt, 2011.
―――. *How We Believe.* New York: Freeman, 1999.
Silver, Mitchell. *A Plausible God: Secular Reflections on Liberal Jewish Theology.* New York: Fordham University Press, 2006.
Skinner, B. F. *The Behavior of Organisms: An Experimental Analysis.* Englewood Cliffs, NJ: Prentice-Hall, 1938.
Soskice, Janet M. *Metaphor and Religious Language.* Oxford, UK: Oxford University Press, 2002.
Stenger, Victor. *God: The Failed Hypothesis.* Amherst, NY: Prometheus, 2007.
―――. *The New Atheism.* Amherst, NY: Prometheus, 2009.
Stevens, S. S. *Handbook of Experimental Psychology.* New York: Wiley, 1951.
Swinburne, Richard. *Epistemic Justification.* Oxford, UK: Clarendon, 2001.
―――. *The Existence of God,* 2nd ed. Oxford, UK: Clarendon, 2010.
Weiner, Norbert. *God and Golem Incorporated.* Cambridge, MA: MIT Press, 1964.
Wilbur, Kenneth. *The Marriage of Sense and Soul.* New York: Random House, 1998.
Wilson, Edward O. *Consilience.* New York: Knopf, 1998.

Woodruff, Paul. *Reverence: Renewing a Forgotten Virtue*. New York: Oxford University Press, 2002.

Wright, Robert. *The Evolution of God*. New York: Little, Brown and Company, 2009.

Zahorik, P., and R. L. Jenison. "Presence as Being-in-the-World." *Presence: Teleoperators and Virtual Environments* 7 (1998): 78–89.

INDEX

ABOUT THE AUTHOR

Thomas B. Sheridan is Ford Professor of Engineering and Applied Psychology Emeritus in the Department of Mechanical Engineering and the Department of Aeronautics and Astronautics at the Massachusetts Institute of Technology (MIT). He was coeditor of the MIT Press journal *Presence: Teleoperators and Virtual Environments*, and served on several editorial boards. He also was editor of *IEEE Transactions on Man-Machine Systems*. Six of his books specialize in human-automation interaction. Sheridan chaired the National Research Council's Committee on Human Factors and has served on numerous government and industrial advisory committees. He was president of the Human Factors Society and is a member of the National Academy of Engineering.